Tell It on the Mountain

INTERFACES

Series Editor: Barbara Green, O.P.

# Tell It on the Mountain

## The Daughter of Jephthah in Judges 11

*Barbara Miller*

A Michael Glazier Book

**LITURGICAL PRESS**

Collegeville, Minnesota

www.litpress.org

A Michael Glazier Book published by Liturgical Press.

Cover design by Ann Blattner. Watercolor by Ethel Boyle.

The author is grateful to the parties listed below for permission to reprint copyrighted texts from:

Roman & Littlefield, *Genesis Rabbah,* Judaic Commentary Series.

*The Old Testament Pseudepigrapha,* vol. II by James H. Charlesworth, ed., copyright © 1985 by James H. Charlesworth. Used by permission of Doubleday, a division of Random House, Inc.

*Targum Pseudo-Jonathan of the Former Prophets,* Liturgical Press, 1987.

University of Delaware Press, poem by Peter Abelard in Wilber Owen Sypherd's *Jephthah's Daughter: A Study in Comparative Literature.*

Poem by Alicia Ostriker, "Rain Falls on the Mountaintop" in *On the Cutting Edge,* Continuum, 2004.

The Scripture quotations contained herein are from the New Revised Standard Version Bible, Catholic Anglicized Edition, © 1999, 1995, 1989, Division of Christian Education of the National Council of the Churches of Christ in the United States of America, and are used by permission. All rights reserved.

1     2     3     4     5     6     7     8     9

**Library of Congress Cataloging-in-Publication Data**

Miller, Barbara, 1942–
    Tell it on the mountain : the daughter of Jephthah in Judges 11 / Barbara Miller.
        p.   cm. — (Interfaces)
    "A Michael Glazier book."
    Summary: "A consideration of Jephthah's daughter in Judges 11–12:7, using feminist and midrashic interpretations"—Provided by publisher.
    Includes bibliographical references and index.
    ISBN-13: 978-0-8146-5843-7 (pbk. : alk. paper)
    ISBN-10: 0-8146-5843-1 (pbk. : alk. paper)
        1. Jephthah's daughter (Biblical figure)   2. Bible. O.T. Judges XI, 1-XII, 7—Criticism, interpretation, etc., Jewish.   3. Bible. O.T. Judges XI, 1-XII, 7—Feminist criticism.   4. Midrash.   I. Title.   II. Series: Interfaces (Collegeville, Minn.)

BS580.J36M55 2005
222'.3206—dc22

                                                                    2005004342

*Dedicated to*
*Sarah, David, Adam, and Aaron MacLeod*

# CONTENTS

# PREFACE

The book you hold in your hand is one of fifteen volumes in an expanding set of volumes. This series, called INTERFACES, is a curriculum adventure, a creative opportunity in teaching and learning, presented at this moment in the long story of how the Bible has been studied, interpreted, and appropriated.

The INTERFACES project was prompted by a number of experiences that you, perhaps, share. When I first taught undergraduates, the college had just received a substantial grant from the National Endowment for the Humanities, and one of the recurring courses designed within the grant was called Great Figures in Pursuit of Excellence. Three courses would be taught, each centering on a figure from some academic discipline or other, with a common seminar section to provide occasion for some integration. Some triads were more successful than others, as you might imagine. But the opportunity to concentrate on a single individual—whether historical or literary—to team teach, to make links to another pair of figures, and to learn new things about other disciplines was stimulating and fun for all involved. A second experience that gave rise to this series came at the same time, connected as well with undergraduates. It was my frequent experience to have Roman Catholic students feel quite put out about taking "more" biblical studies, since, as they confidently affirmed, they had already been there many times and done it all. That was, of course, not true; as we well know, there is always more to learn. And often those who felt most informed were the least likely to take on new information when offered it.

A stimulus as primary as my experience with students was the familiarity of listening to friends and colleagues at professional meetings talking about the research that excites us most. I often wondered: Do her undergraduate students know about this? Or how does he bring these ideas—clearly so energizing to him—into the college classroom? Perhaps some of us have felt bored with classes that seem wholly unrelated to research, that rehash the same familiar material repeatedly. Hence the idea for this series of books to bring to the fore and combine some of our research interests with our teaching and learning. Accordingly, this series is not so much about creating texts *for* student audiences but rather about *sharing* our scholarly passions with them. Because these volumes are intended each as a piece of original scholarship, they are geared to be stimulating to both students and established scholars, perhaps resulting in some fruitful collaborative learning adventures.

The series also developed from a widely shared sense that all academic fields are expanding and exploding, and that to contemplate "covering" even a testament (let alone the whole Bible or western monotheistic religions) needs to be abandoned in favor of something with greater depth and fresh focus. At the same time, the links between our fields are becoming increasingly obvious as well, and the possibilities for study which draw together academic realms that had once seemed separate is exciting. Finally, the spark of enthusiasm that almost always ignited when I mentioned to students and colleagues the idea of single figures in combination—interfacing—encouraged me that this was an idea worth trying.

And so with the leadership and help of Liturgical Press Academic Editor Linda Maloney, as well as with the encouragement and support of Editorial Director Mark Twomey, the series has begun to take shape.

Each volume in the INTERFACES series focuses clearly on a biblical character (or perhaps a pair of them). The characters from the first set of volumes are in some cases powerful—King Saul, Pontius Pilate—and familiar—John the Baptist, Jeremiah; in other cases they will strike you as minor and little-known—the Cannibal Mothers, Herodias. The second "litter" I added notables of various ranks and classes: Jezebel, queen of the Northern Israelite realm; James of Jerusalem and "brother of the Lord"; Simon the Pharisee, dinner host to Jesus; Legion, the Gerasene demoniac encountered so dramatically by Jesus. In this third set we find a similar contrast between apparently mighty and marginal characters: the prophet Jonah who speaks a few powerfully efficacious words; ben Sira, sage in late second temple Judah; and less powerful but perhaps an even greater reading challenge stand Jephthah's daughter and Ezekiel's wife. In any case, each of them has been chosen to open up a set of worlds for consideration. The named (or unnamed) character interfaces with his or her historical-cultural world and its many issues, with other characters from biblical literature; each character has drawn forth the creativity of the author, who has taken on the challenge of engaging many readers. The books are designed for college students (though we think suitable for seminary courses and for serious Bible study), planned to provide young adults with relevant information and at a level of critical sophistication that matches the rest of the undergraduate curriculum.

In fact, the expectation is that what students are learning in other classes of historiography, literary theory, and cultural anthropology will find an echo in these books, each of which is explicit about at least two relevant methodologies. To engage at least two significant methods with some thoroughness is challenging to do. Implicit in this task is the sense that it is not possible to do all methods with depth; when several volumes of the series are used together, a balance will emerge for readers. It is surely the case that biblical studies is in a methodology-conscious moment, and the INTERFACES series embraces it enthusiastically. Our hope is for students to continue to see the relationship between their best questions and their most valuable insights, between how they approach texts and what they find there. The volumes go well beyond familiar paraphrase of narratives to ask questions that are relevant in our era. At the same time, the series authors also have each dealt with the notion of the Bible as Scripture in a way condign for them. None of the books is preachy or hortatory, and yet the self-implicating aspects of working with the revelatory text are handled frankly. The assumption is, again, that college can be a good time for people to reexamine and rethink their beliefs and assumptions, and they need to do so in good company.

The INTERFACES volumes all challenge teachers to revision radically the scope of a course, to allow the many connections among characters to serve as its warp and weft. What would emerge fresh if a Deuteronomistic History class were organized around King Saul, Queen Jezebel, and the two women who petitioned their nameless monarch? How is Jesus' ministry thrown into fresh relief when structured by shared concerns implied by a demoniac, a Pharisee, James—a disciple and John the Baptist—a mentor? And for those who must "do it all" in one semester, a study of Genesis' Joseph, Herodias and Pontius Pilate might allow for a timely foray into postcolonialism. With whom would you now place the long-suffering but doughty wife of Ezekiel: with the able Jezebel, or with the apparently celibate Jonah? Or perhaps with Herodias? Would Jephthah's daughter organize an excellent course with the Cannibal Mothers, and perhaps as well with the Gerasene demoniac, as fresh and under-heard voices speak their words to the powerful? Would you study monarchy effectively by working with bluebloods Jezebel and Saul, as they contend with their opponents, whether those resemble John the Baptist or Pontius Pilate? Depending on the needs of your courses and students, these rich and diverse character studies will offer you many options.

The INTERFACES volumes are not substitutes for the Bible. In every case, they are to be read with the text. Quoting has been kept to a minimum, for that very reason. The series is accompanied by a straightforward companion, *From Earth's Creation* to John's *Revelation: The INTERFACES Biblical Storyline Companion,* which provides a quick overview of the whole storyline into which the characters under special study fit. The companion is available gratis for those using two or more of the INTERFACES volumes. Already readers of diverse proficiency and familiarity have registered satisfaction with this slim overview narrated by biblical Sophia.

The series challenge—for publisher, writers, teachers, and students—is to combine the volumes creatively, to INTERFACE them well so that the vast potential of the biblical text continues to unfold for us all. These volumes offer a foretaste of other volumes currently on the drawing board. It has been a pleasure to work with the authors of these volumes as well as with the series consultants: Carleen Mandolfo for Hebrew Bible and Catherine Murphy for New Testament. It is the hope of all of us that you will find the series useful and stimulating for your own teaching and learning.

> Barbara Green, O.P.
> INTERFACES Series Editor
> May 16, 2005
> Berkeley, California

# ACKNOWLEDGMENTS

I want to express my appreciation to colleagues, students, and friends who have shared my interest in the narrative of Jephthah's daughter. Thanks go to Gerda Lerner for her compositional advice, encouragement, and inspiration; Cynthia Miller for critiquing the manuscript; Larry Kohn for help with rabbinic interpretation; and Jonathan Schofer for bibliographic assistance.

I am also grateful to Edgewood College for funding my sabbatical, which enabled me to concentrate fully on this project.

I want to thank students in my biblical studies classes who composed midrash for the final chapter of this book, especially K. Ritchie Rheaume, Gloria Alt, and Ann Krummel. Long-time friend Susan Hansen contributed midrash and read the manuscript.

Barbara Green, editor of the INTERFACES series, encouraged me to contribute to this project and provided valuable critique. Thanks also to Linda Maloney, Liturgical Press Academic Editor and Janet Josvai for providing the index.

Jane Schaberg and Pamela Milne have made my career in biblical studies possible. Jane's teaching and careful analysis of feminist themes in the Bible inspired my imagination. Pamela's assistance and encouragement have been integral to my work.

My most profound thanks go to Patricia Meloy for her enthusiasm for this project and careful stylistic editing. Her interest in and knowledge of the subject matter were invaluable. Our sometimes-animated conversations guided the shape of this work.

Barbara Miller

# INTRODUCTION
## *A Tale of Violence*

This INTERFACES volume focuses on a tale of violence in which a young woman is sacrificed as a burnt offering by her father because of a hasty vow he had made to the LORD. We will convene an imaginary gathering of twenty-first-century feminist biblical scholars, medieval rabbis, and current-day readers to discuss this nearly three thousand-year-old biblical narrative. What values will each bring to the discussion? Will there be consensus on some issues but disagreement on others? Our task is to bring these voices together and engage them in a conversation about justice, loyalty, power, and God.

The narrative of Jephthah and his unnamed daughter is found in Judges 11:1–12:7. Jephthah was the son of Gilead, a warrior, and an unnamed woman described as a prostitute. (Gilead was also the name of Jephthah's region.) As a youth he was driven away from home by his stepbrothers and joined a company of outlaws engaged in raiding. Eventually the elders of Gilead called Jephthah back to lead negotiations with the Ammonite enemy. Efforts to negotiate peace proved futile, and war broke out. The narrative continues:

> Then the spirit of the LORD came upon Jephthah, and he passed through Gilead and Manasseh. He passed on to Mizpah of Gilead, and from Mizpah of Gilead he passed on to the Ammonites. And Jephthah made a vow to the LORD, and said, "If you will give the Ammonites into my hand, then whoever comes out of the doors of my house to meet me, when I return victorious from the Ammonites, shall be the LORD's to be offered up by me as a burnt offering." So Jephthah crossed over to the Ammonites to fight against them; and the LORD gave them into his hand. He inflicted a massive defeat on them from Aroer to the neighborhood of Minnith, twenty towns, and as far as Abel-keramim.

So the Ammonites were subdued before the people of Israel. (Judg 11:29-33)[1]

The next section of the narrative introduces Jephthah's daughter and describes the circumstances surrounding her death.

Then Jephthah came to his home at Mizpah; and there was his daughter coming out to meet him with timbrels and with dancing. She was his only child; he had no son or daughter except her. When he saw her, he tore his clothes, and said, "Alas, my daughter! You have brought me very low; you have become the cause of great trouble to me. For I have opened my mouth to the LORD, and cannot take back my vow." She said to him, "My father, if you have opened your mouth to the LORD, do to me according to what has gone out of your mouth, now that the LORD has given you vengeance against your enemies, the Ammonites." And she said to her father, "Let this thing be done for me: Grant me two months, so that I may go and wander on the mountains, and bewail my virginity, my companions and I." "Go," he said and sent her away for two months. So she departed, she and her companions, and bewailed her virginity on the mountains. At the end of two months she returned to her father, who did with her according to the vow he had made. She had never slept with a man. So there arose an Israelite custom that for four days every year the daughters of Israel would go out to lament the daughter of Jephthah the Gileadite. (Judg 11:34-40)

Following his daughter's death Jephthah engaged in civil war with the tribe of Ephraim and later died after ruling as a judge in Israel for six years (Judg 12:1-7).

This narrative is not widely read or studied. For many it is too violent and simply too outmoded for the twenty-first century. Why read about a father killing his daughter? Why study a story in which God seems to withdraw from human tragedy? Isn't there enough violence in today's world without reading about it in the Bible? And yet it is because we are bombarded by violence daily that we can benefit from using this narrative to question the unjust political systems and power struggles that foster it.

To begin this study we need first to understand the book of Judges in the context of the Bible as a whole, to situate the Jephthah narrative within Judges, and to appreciate the role of a judge in ancient Israel.

---

[1] Unless otherwise stated, biblical quotations are from the *New Revised Standard Version (NRSV)*.

## Placement of the Book of Judges in the Bible

The Tanakh (Hebrew Bible), which Christians refer to as the Old Testament, contains three major divisions—Torah (Genesis, Exodus, Leviticus, Numbers, and Deuteronomy), Prophets (Former and Latter Prophets), and Writings.[2] Judges is found among the Former Prophets, following the book of Joshua. It purports to deal with the period termed "the tribal confederacy" (1200–1000 B.C.E.), when the Hebrews had returned to Canaan after their enslavement in Egypt and forty years of wandering in the wilderness of Sinai under Moses' leadership.

The entry into the Promised Land of Canaan was the culmination of a theophany (manifestation of God) to Moses in which God told Moses that God would deliver the Hebrews out of slavery in Egypt and bring them "to a good and broad land, a land flowing with milk and honey" (Exod 3:8). Once in Canaan, the Hebrews acquired portions of land that were named, for the most part, after the sons of Jacob. From north to south the tribes included Asher, Naphtali, Dan, Zebulun, Issachar, Manasseh, Ephraim, Gad, Reuben, Benjamin, and Judah.[3] Gilead, the location of the Jephthah narrative, lay in the territory of Manasseh and Gad in the mountainous Transjordan region. The battle depicted in Judges 11 between Gilead and the Ammonites situates Ammon to the east of Gad.

The editor of Judges assesses the governance of the tribes during this period a failure. The book ends with the statement: "In those days there was no king in Israel; all the people did what was right in their own eyes" (Judg 21:25). Later, in an attempt to rectify this failure, Israel would adopt a monarchical form of governance, which had its own failings.

---

[2] The Tanakh differs from the Christian Old Testament in the order and categories given to its books. In Tanakh, the Former Prophets include Joshua, Judges, 1 and 2 Samuel, and 1 and 2 Kings. In the Christian Bible these are the historical books. The Latter Prophets of the Tanakh are called writing prophets in the Christian Bible, such as Isaiah, Jeremiah, Ezekiel, Hosea, Joel, Amos, Obadiah, Jonah, Micah, Nahum, Habakkuk, Zephaniah, Haggai, Zechariah, and Malachi. The Writings in the Tanakh include Psalms, Proverbs, Job, Ruth, Song of Songs, Ecclesiastes, Lamentations, Esther, Daniel, Ezra, Nehemiah, and 1 and 2 Chronicles. The Tanakh places the Prophets before the Writings, while the Christian Bible places them after the Writings. The Tanakh ends with Ezra, Nehemiah, and Chronicles, all books related to the return from the Babylonian exile.

[3] There is no tribe bearing Joseph's name directly. Instead two tribes, Ephraim and Manasseh, are named for Joseph's sons. The tribe of Levi had no allotment of land in Canaan (Josh 13:33), a fact attributed to the massacre that Levi and Simeon carried out in Shechem (Gen 34:25-29). According to Gen 49:5-7, the tribes of Simeon and Levi were scattered throughout Israel. Later, Levites constituted a part of the Temple priesthood and derived their support from offerings brought by the Israelites.

## Placement of Jephthah's Story within the Book of Judges

Judges begins with an introduction describing the military successes and failures of the tribes after the death of Joshua (Judg 1:1–3:6). A second section contains narratives of the deeds of the major and minor judges: Othniel, Ehud, Samgar, Deborah, Gideon, Abimelech, Tola, Jair, Jephthah, Ibzan, Elon, Abdon, and Samson (Judg 3:7–16:31). The third section portrays the situation of anarchy prior to the establishment of the monarchy in 1 Samuel (Judg 17:1–21:25).[4]

The narratives of the judges are thought by some scholars to have been edited by the Deuteronomistic editor, who frames them within a theology of disobedience and obedience. When the Israelites are disobedient and abandon God, God gives them over to their enemies and they suffer defeat. When Israel cries out to God for relief from oppression, God raises up judges who are successful in battle against the enemies and brings the people once again into a covenant relationship with God. After the judge dies, the cycle of disobedience, oppression, deliverance, and obedience begins again. While this framework appears rather simplistic, it reflects a broader theme in Torah and in the prophets depicting Israel as ever straying from and being called back to God.

Prior to Jephthah's leadership the Israelites once again had fallen into idolatry and consequently suffered defeat at the hands of the Philistines and the Ammonites. Israel cried out to God for relief and was reminded that in the past they had been delivered from a long line of oppressors, including the Egyptians, Amorites, Ammonites, Amalekites, and Maonites. This time God threatened not to deliver them and taunted them with instructions to cry for help to the gods (idols) they were worshiping. The Israelites repented with the words: "We have sinned; do to us whatever seems good to you; but deliver us this day," and God relented (Judg 10:14-16). Within this context Jephthah is recruited to defeat the Ammonites. He is successful and judges Israel for six years.

The successful tribal leadership developed under Deborah and Gideon diminishes after Jephthah's rule. While he is successful in battle, he sacrifices his daughter and foments intertribal warfare. In the eyes of the Deuteronomistic editor, the moral fiber of Israel degenerates, culminating in a grisly story of rape, dismemberment, and civil war, paving the way for the establishment of the monarchy.[5]

---

[4] For a more detailed outline that also highlights the women mentioned in Judges see Gale Yee, ed., *Judges and Method: New Approaches in Biblical Studies* (Minneapolis: Fortress, 1995) 3.

[5] According to the Documentary Hypothesis, the Deuteronomist edited Deuteronomy, Joshua, Judges, 1 and 2 Samuel and 1 and 2 Kings. See Chapter One for further information.

The individual narratives assembled in Judges probably arose as oral tradition about individual tribes and their military opponents. At some stage the narratives came to speak of Israel as a whole rather than as individual tribes. Most likely the final form of the book was composed more than four hundred years after the time of the judges, the failed monarchy, and the Babylonian exile. Various stages of Deuteronomistic editing ensued, producing the form that appears in the Bible.[6]

## What Is a Judge?

The term "judge" is an English translation of the Hebrew word *šopet,* which refers primarily to military leaders mentioned in the book of Judges. The noun "judge" occurs in Judg 2:16-17 to speak of leaders the LORD appoints to deliver Israelites from their enemies. The people do not listen to the judges, but return to their previous practice of worshiping idols. The only other use of the noun "judge" occurs in Judg 11:27, to refer to the LORD. At the end of Jephthah's negotiations with the Ammonites he says that it is the LORD who is judge, deciding whether Israel or the Ammonites will be victorious in the subsequent battle. Other uses of the root *(špt)* refer to a variety of governing activities performed by the leaders.[7]

The chronological sequence of the judges and the historicity of the narratives in Judges continue to be debated. Deborah is the only woman mentioned in the powerful role of a judge. For the most part these charismatic leaders fought enemy armies who invaded tribal territories. Deborah was the only one who rendered judicial decisions as well as serving as a prophet and a military commander. Jephthah, though a judge, functioned as a political emissary and commander of military forces. Both Deborah and Jephthah had experiences of God.

## The Purpose of this Book

Rather than concentrating on the complex historical aspects of the period of the Judges, in this book we will enter into a literary analysis that permits the reader to dialogue with the text. Readers are invited to engage in a detailed reading of Judg 11:29-40 that focuses on the narrator's plot

[6] Gale Yee, ed., *Judges and Method,* 7–12. Also see Frank Moore Cross, *Canaanite Myth and Hebrew Epic: Essays in the Religion of Israel* (Cambridge, MA: Harvard University Press, 1973) 274–89, and Richard Elliott Friedman, *The Exile and Biblical Narrative: The Formation of the Deuteronomistic and Priestly Works* (Chico: Scholars, 1981).

[7] For a description of "savior," another term used in connection with the judges, see Robert G. Boling, *Judges,* AB 6a (Garden City, NY: Doubleday, 1975) 5.

development and portrayal of characters. This will enable the reader to distinguish between what is actually stated in the narrative, what the narrator leaves unsaid, and how these work together.

As background to a literary analysis we will discuss some historical aspects of Judg 11:29-40 as they inform a general understanding of the text and serve as a basis for a woman-centered or feminist analysis. For the most part we will accept the narrative of Jephthah's daughter as it appears in its final form in the Bible. The goal of our literary analysis is to allow the reader to enter into dialogue with the text by noting the point of view of the narrator, development of plot, and portrayal of the characters. This type of reading enables one to distinguish between what the narrator actually says and what is left unsaid. In other words, what is not stated in the narrative is nearly as important as what is stated. These narrative gaps offer opportunities for readers to dialogue with the text, particularly about related values.

Two methods of biblical analysis will be used to enhance this study, namely midrashic or rabbinic interpretation and feminist interpretation. The term *midrash* (plural: *midrashim*) can refer to a process of interpretation or to the collections of this type of writing as composed by medieval rabbis. Jewish scholars recognized that over time questions arose concerning the significance of particular parts of the Bible. In an effort to update the Bible for changing social, political, and religious circumstances the rabbis wrote commentary either as case law or as story. We will be concerned with narrative midrash, that is, the technique of embellishing a biblical narrative with another narrative that fills gaps in the story to illustrate a point for a new generation. For example, in the Middle Ages the rabbis were concerned that too many people were making vows that they were unable to keep. The Jephthah narrative in which Jephthah makes a vow that brings about disaster serves as a focal point for midrash or new stories that stress the need for caution in making vows. Such a midrash or interpretative story could portray Jephthah consulting with others about the obligation of keeping a vow that involves the loss of a human life. This new story might offer alternatives missing in the original narrative. Thus midrash updates the debate about vows in later social circumstances.

Collections of rabbinic interpretation are referred to as "The Midrash." Multiple collections of these writings have been gathered in various volumes. There is no one volume that contains all the midrash. Midrash from a variety of sources, ancient and modern, are collected in the appendix of this book. Some of these texts have only recently been translated into English.

The second method of biblical analysis, referred to as "feminist interpretation," arises out of the modern feminist movement that recognizes that women have been subordinated to men in virtually all cultures throughout time. Feminism seeks the equality of men and women in all aspects of life. A feminist interpretation of the Bible claims that the Bible was written in androcentric (male-centered) cultures, and that, for the most part, this cultural overlay has been used to keep women in subordinate roles. Feminist interpreters study narratives, such as that of Jephthah's daughter, noting the obvious male domination in the stories and recognizing the brief references to the world of women. For example, while traditional biblical interpretation has focused on Jephthah as the protagonist in our story, feminist interpretation focuses on the daughter. The daughter is a pivotal character who, while portrayed as a victim, becomes the one who exposes the power inequity behind the story.

Feminist criticism acknowledges that female characters are largely created by male writers who inscribe the social expectations of their day upon the characters. Thus Jephthah's daughter is sympathetic with her father's plight and agrees to the sacrifice. Feminist criticism also attempts to highlight the woman's voice. In this narrative the daughter has a voice and asks her father for time away with her friends before her death. Her two-month respite invites feminist readers to imagine an unstated prolonged conversation among the women. At this point feminist interpretation intersects with midrash.

Our goal in this book is to create a conversation between medieval rabbis and feminist interpreters over the values that emerge from their approaches to the text. Although both groups are concerned with justice, loyalty, and compassion, each approaches these values from a different perspective. Our study will look beyond these two groups by introducing a third party, the modern writer of midrash. Modern voices will join the discussion by articulating values that update this biblical story for the twenty-first century.

## Overview

Chapter One opens with an examination of certain key Israelite beliefs and practices that are essential for understanding Judges 11, including a discussion of the role of women in ancient Israel. This chapter also offers a strategy for a literary reading of biblical narrative, which involves color coding the text to facilitate recognition of various elements of the narrative such as setting, characters, plot development, and resolution of tension. Another strategy for determining the point of view of the narrator invites the reader to retell the narrative from the point of view of other characters in the text. This technique can highlight the muted voices that lie at the margins of the story and that may differ significantly from the narrator's emphasis. The chapter closes with a strategy for recognizing narrative silences or gaps that serve as entry points for midrash.

Chapter Two describes the medieval rabbis' development of biblical interpretation. The Mishnah, Talmud, and collections of midrash served to update ancient teachings as time passed. For example, the legal status of a vow is key to the Jephthah story, so we will trace the traditions related to the making and keeping of vows through these rabbinic texts. Our primary concern will be narrative midrash that fills gaps in biblical stories. Midrash is a vehicle for creating a dialogue with the Bible even today.

The rabbis often read a biblical story in light of another biblical story. The Jephthah narrative has much in common with the story of Abraham offering his son Isaac as a sacrifice (Gen 22:1-19). This type of critique, termed intertextual reading, notes similar plot lines, thematic ideas, repetition of words, or character traits in the stories. It helps a reader discern a greater number of possibilities than a single text offers.[8] One text can echo an element in the other text or one text can point out a narrative silence in the other text. The rabbis used an adaptation of this method to create their midrashic interpretations of biblical narratives. Chapter Two proposes an intertextual reading of the Abraham and Jephthah narratives and illustrates the intertextual quality of the accompanying midrash.

Chapter Three focuses on the role of feminist critique. Feminist interpretation views the text from the perspective of women as marginalized characters. While feminist interpretation originated with white, educated, Western, middle-class women in the 1970s, it has now expanded to include the critiques of African-American, Mujerista/Latina, and Jewish women, among others. Examples from each of these perspectives highlight the particular social location and concerns of the interpreter. We illustrate each of these interpretations with appropriate biblical narratives featuring women. We close with a discussion of the creation narrative contained in Genesis 2 and 3, which, according to many feminists, inscribes a subordinate position for women in societies. This single narrative and its interpretations speak of the need for a reassessment of texts, such as the Jephthah story, that highlight the injustice done to women.

Chapter Four contains traditional midrash on Judges 11. We have arranged the various midrashic stories in thematic categories that reflect concerns of the rabbis. For example, the rabbis are disturbed that Jephthah

---

[8] Ellen van Wolde, "Intertextuality: Ruth in Dialogue with Tamar," in Athalya Brenner and Carole Fontaine, eds., *A Feminist Companion to Reading the Bible* (Sheffield: Sheffield Academic Press, 1997) 431.

did not explore alternatives to carrying out his vow. In their midrash they discuss his options and even postulate options for his daughter. They claim that Jephthah could have consulted with a priest and that the daughter actually attempted to consult authorities. The rabbis are also concerned with the apparent absence of God as the narrative progresses toward the death of the daughter. This issue has wider implications as the rabbis move away from an image of God intervening in situations to a focus on human responsibility. This collection of midrash is varied, and at times it contains conflicting opinions that indicate the fluid nature of rabbinic debate.

Chapter Five presents critiques of feminist interpreters who read the Jephthah text as a violent story in which patriarchal authority operates at the expense of a female victim. As in Chapter Four, the comments of feminist writers are arranged in categories that reflect the writers' concerns. For example, is the daughter a hero or a victim? Some see her as a hero in her decision to uphold her father's vow at any cost. Others claim that she was a victim, trapped by her father's unnecessary vow and a lack of options for appeal. Another issue that concerns the feminists is the sketchy description of the time the women spend on the mountain. It leaves us with many questions about their activities. Some writers propose that a rite of passage for pubescent girls might have been the basis of the story. As support for this interpretation the writers recall Greek legends containing myth and rituals for such occasions.

Feminist interpretation, like that of the rabbis, makes use of silences in the original narrative. Neither interpretation provides historical answers to questions. However, both offer opportunities for discussing values.

Chapter Six presents a dialogue between the medieval rabbis and modern feminists about values. Justice, loyalty, compassion, respect for tradition, and responsibility are values held by each group. Because each speaks from a different historical setting, their interpretation of these values differs to some degree. At the heart of this discussion is the role of God in human affairs. Each group attempts to deal with how God is present in the struggle for justice.

Chapter Seven presents modern midrash on Judges 11. My students and friends were invited to identify narrative silences in the story and to compose midrash that reflected their own experience of the text. Of major concern were family relationships, friendships, and a call for social action against abuse. This chapter represents a collaborative effort in which multiple modern voices have joined in a conversation about a violent story in a sacred text. The modern conversation is mediated by the efforts of medieval rabbis and feminist interpreters who, like today's writers, are concerned about God's call for justice.

The appendix to this book contains English translations of rabbinic and some modern midrash on Judges 11. Because many of these sources are difficult to find, they are reproduced here as a resource for the reader. The writings are arranged chronologically insofar as possible given the controversies about dating the texts.

Jephthah's daughter and her companions spent two months on the mountain coming to terms with her impending death at the hands of her father. The multi-generational conversation contained in this book challenges readers to continue the life-affirming call for justice and to *Tell It on the Mountain*.

## A Personal Note

It is important for readers of this book to understand the point of view of its writer. Feminist interpreters traditionally identify themselves with respect to their social location and experience. Thus I wish to identify myself as a white American woman, a feminist, a professor of biblical studies at a liberal arts college in the Midwest, the mother of a daughter and grandmother of two grandsons (to whom this book is dedicated), a widow, and a Jew by conversion in the Reform tradition. I offer this self-description as an acknowledgment that my work is both enriched by and limited by the experiences of my lifetime.

# CHAPTER ONE

## Beginning the Conversation

This opening chapter is concerned primarily with a literary approach to the narrative of Jephthah's daughter. Historical material pertinent to the narrative will be supplied at various points, but we will be assuming the historicity of the Deuteronomistic framework. Literary criticism differs from historical criticism of the Bible in that it is concerned with the interaction of setting, plot, and character development within a narrative rather than the historical veracity of place names and the chronology of events. Literary criticism accepts the given text without critiquing the history of the editing or the redaction of the text. It involves a synchronic approach, which views a complex of events that occur within particular time periods, rather than using a diachronic approach, which involves historical progression across time.

Literary analysis does not take place in a vacuum. History and an appreciation for the composition of a final text serve as a background for most forms of biblical analysis. The historical setting of Judges is outlined below to assist the reader with the literary study that follows. For a broader picture of the biblical story we recommend the introductory volume of this series, *From Earth's Creation to John's Revelation,* by Barbara Green, Carleen Mandolfo, and Catherine M. Murphy.

## A Historical Approach to the Bible

Beginning in the nineteenth century, when scholars adopted a historical approach to the Bible, understanding the historical setting and the customs of a given biblical text has been considered key to biblical study. This approach considers the historical circumstances surrounding the text, its authorship, and its date of composition. Historical analysis of a particular biblical text is closely related to a form of literary criticism known as source criticism (or source analysis).[1] Source criticism acknowledges that larger units of the Bible are made up of various smaller units or sources that were later edited into books of the Bible or a collection of books, such as the Torah. Julius Wellhausen is credited with developing the documentary hypothesis that identifies at least four sources within the Torah—Yahwist, Elohist, Priestly, and Deuteronomistic.[2] The book of Judges is a collection of individual narratives about various judges that appears to have been assembled and edited by the Deuteronomistic editors. These editors probably wrote after 620 B.C.E., long after the historical period of the judges and well after the failure of the monarchy. Most likely the book was completed between 587 and 398 B.C.E.[3] The editors interpreted the narratives of the individual judges and the monarchy to say that the failure of these two forms of governance was due to the disobedience of the people.

What can be said about the historical veracity of biblical narrative? It is safe to say that the Bible offers clues to presumed historical settings in the ancient world. Judges 11 mentions geographical locations such as Gilead, Manasseh, Mizpah, Aroer, Minnith, and Abel-keramim. Although the citing of specific place names seems to lend historical creditability to the narrative, archaeologists debate the location of some of the towns. For example, the location of Mizpah is unknown.[4] The questionable authenticity of place names may be jarring to modern readers, leading them to discredit the narrative as a whole. However, modern biblical criticism suggests that the value of a narrative, or indeed the entire Bible, lies not in pinpointing

[1] For a concise description of literary criticism see Carl H. Holladay, "Biblical Criticism," *Harper's Bible Dictionary* (San Francisco: HarperSanFrancisco, 1985) 131; John Barton, "Source Criticism," in David Noel Freedman, ed., *The Anchor Bible Dictionary (ABD)* (New York: Doubleday, 1992) 6:162.

[2] The historical- and source-critical approach to the Bible was seen as a corrective to previous approaches that interpreted the Bible through Jewish and Christian post-biblical theologies. For example, the salvation history approach viewed the entire Bible, both Old and New Testaments, as a linear timeline in which the progression of events in the Tanakh served primarily as a backdrop for the culmination of salvation in the person of Jesus. Julius Wellhausen's source theory shifted the focus away from particular theological interpretations to how the text itself developed.

[3] For a discussion of various methods of interpretation offering clues to a date for the final form of Judges see Gale A. Yee, ed., *Judges and Method: New Approaches in Biblical Studies* (Minneapolis: Fortress, 1995) 5.

[4] According to Robert G. Boling, Aroer, Minnith, and Abel-keramim were located in the western part of Rabbath-ammon, but their exact location is not known. Boling, *Judges*, AB 6A (Garden City, NY: Doubleday, 1975) 208.

actual historical settings and events but in a search for broader themes that reveal important truths about the relationship between God and human beings.

Although biblical narratives leave many historical and geographical questions unanswered, they can be substantiated by archaeological findings. For example, when Jephthah makes a vow that whatever or whoever *(asher)* comes forth from his house will be offered as a burnt offering to the LORD, the reader may wonder what constituted a house during this period and who inhabited it. Archaeologists describe houses from 1200–1000 B.C.E. as four-room, two-story structures. The first level of the house was probably used for housing animals and storing food, while the second level contained living quarters for an extended family.[5] Since animals lived on the lower level of the houses, Jephthah may have expected a goat or other small animal to come forth first from the dwelling upon his return. Archaeological data thus leaves the translation of *asher* (the object of sacrifice) open to whatever or whoever came out of the house.

An analysis of Judges 11 requires understanding ancient practices and beliefs in Israel insofar as is possible. Four of these will be treated here: the Spirit of the LORD, the nature of an Israelite vow, the concept of sacrifice in Israel, particularly human sacrifice, and the role of women in ancient Israel.

## Spirit of the LORD

The Spirit *(ruah,* meaning "breath" or "wind") of the LORD, as presented in Judges, Samuel, Kings, and the prophets, refers to God's power or inspiration that comes upon an individual and enables one to exhibit great courage or wisdom. In Judges the Spirit of the LORD is a source of strength enabling military victory.

Othniel, Gideon, Samson, and Jephthah are said to have experienced the Spirit of the LORD coming upon them prior to engaging in battle. When the Spirit of the LORD comes upon the judge Othniel he goes out to war, and the LORD gives the king of Aram into his hand (Judg 3:10). There is peace for forty years until Othniel dies. The Spirit of the LORD takes possession of Gideon when he is faced with war with the Midianites and Amalekites (Judg 6:34). Gideon rallies support from other tribes to fight the battle. Gideon then seeks the approval of God by placing a golden fleece on the ground for two nights. If the fleece collects dew the first night and remains dry the second night, Gideon will be assured that God will

[5] For a diagram of these houses see Larry G. Herr and Douglas R. Clark, "Excavating the Tribe of Reuben," *BAR* (March/April 2001) 36–47.

bring Gideon victory. After various trials, victory comes and there is peace for forty years. The legend of Samson notes several occasions when the Spirit of the LORD comes upon Samson. In one instance Samson is given the strength to tear apart a lion with his bare hands (Judg 14:6). On another occasion the Spirit of the LORD rushes upon him and he kills thirty men in Ashkelon and takes their spoil (Judg 14:19). Finally, the Spirit of the LORD enables Samson to loosen the ropes binding his arms and to kill a thousand Philistines with the jawbone of a donkey (Judg 15:14-15). Samson judges Israel for twenty years prior to his death.

The Spirit of the LORD comes upon Jephthah just as negotiations with the king of the Ammonites fail (Judg 11:29). Jephthah warns the king that the LORD is the judge who will decide which side will be victorious. The spirit then comes upon Jephthah. Following this he makes a vow that, if he is victorious in battle, whatever or whoever comes out of his house first upon his return from battle will be given to the LORD as a burnt offering. Jephthah is victorious and rules for six years.

Othniel, Gideon, Samson, and Jephthah experience the Spirit of the LORD prior to going into battle and as a result are victorious. Gideon and Jephthah pursue this experience a step further. Gideon seeks a sign from God by means of the golden fleece, while Jephthah takes the situation into his own hands by making a vow. Gideon expects confirmation before going into battle, but Jephthah rashly promises to offer a sacrifice following the battle to affirm God's support. Jephthah, who has patiently negotiated with the enemy in vain, loses patience when he receives the Spirit of the LORD. In making the vow he appears to show a lack of faith in God's ability to bring victory.

The shortness of Jephthah's rule (six years) may imply that he is not honored as a judge, presumably because of his vow and the sacrifice of his daughter. The rule of the other judges was much longer. Othniel and Gideon were said to rule for forty years, which implies a long time rather than a literal number of years. (For example, the Hebrews wandered in the wilderness for "forty years.") The battles in which Othniel and Gideon fought resulted in long periods of peace prior to their deaths. It is implied that length of rule reflects the successful leadership of a judge.

## Vow

In the Tanakh, a vow is a deliberate promise to repay God for God's help, often in the form of a sacrifice. The literary form of a vow consists of a condition (if God will do thus and so) and a promise (then the one making the vow will do thus and so). Like Jephthah, Jacob, the Israelites, Hannah, and Absalom make vows to God, but Jephthah's vow contains an element different from the others.

In Gen 28:20 Jacob vows that if God will be with him and help him on his way, providing food and clothing as he returns to his father's house, then the LORD will be his God. Jacob sets up a stone commemorating the vow, at a place he names Bethel (the house of God), and he promises to tithe, giving back to God one tenth of whatever God gives him. In Num 21:2 Israel vows that if the LORD will grant them military victory over the king of Arad, the Israelites will utterly destroy the king's towns. The utter destruction of the enemy is to be an offering (sacrifice) to the LORD. In 1 Sam 1:11 Hannah makes a vow that if God will grant her a son she will offer her child as a nazirite, i.e., one who will be of special service to God.[6] In 2 Sam 15:7-8 David's son Absalom asks his father to allow him to fulfill a vow he had made while in Geshur. Absalom vowed that if God would allow him to return to Jerusalem he would worship God at Hebron. The conditions set forth in these vows involve safe transport, victory in battle, and a male child. The promise made in fulfillment of each of these vows is a renewed dedication to God. Jacob dedicates a place for worship, Hannah dedicates her son to God's service, and Absalom vows to worship God in another location. The Israelites in Num 21:1-3 offer the defeated enemy as an offering to God. As noted by David Marcus, in each of these four vows there is a direct relation between the condition of the vow and the promise of the vow.[7] Jephthah, however, asks for God's favor in victory without promising renewed dedication to God.

Jephthah's vow differs from the four vows just described. Judg 11:30-31 states that, as Jephthah makes his way to fight the Ammonites, he makes a vow to the LORD: "If you will give the Ammonites into my hand, then whoever comes out of the doors of my house to meet me when I return victorious from the Ammonites shall be the LORD's, to be offered up by me as a burnt offering." The condition asking God to bring military victory, and the promise to offer a burnt offering are much like Israel's situation in Num 21:1-3. There are differences, however: Marcus notes that Jephthah's promise is not directly related to his condition. Israel offers the spoils of the battle at hand, but Jephthah's offering is not directly associated with the battle. His burnt offering is removed from the urgency of the battleground to his victorious arrival at his home.

---

[6] A nazirite vowed to abstain from wine, was not to cut his or her hair, and was not to approach a corpse (see Num 6:1-21). Samuel and Samson are mentioned as nazirites. Both were consecrated prior to birth.

[7] David Marcus, *Jephthah and His Vow* (Lubbock: Texas Tech Press, 1986) 19.

Another similarity pertinent to the vows made by Jacob, Hannah, and Jephthah is their epiphany experience. Jacob dreams of a ladder set up between earth and heaven with angels ascending and descending. The LORD repeats the ancestral promise that Jacob's offspring will possess the land. A distraught Hannah prays for a son in the temple at Shiloh and receives assurance, through the priest Eli, that "the God of Israel will grant the petition she made" for a son (1 Sam 1:17). On the way to battle, Jephthah receives the Spirit of the LORD. Unlike Jacob and Hannah, Jephthah hears no assurance of victory, yet the presence of the Spirit of the LORD implies that he will succeed.

Two gaps are evident in Jephthah's vow that are not evident in the other vows. One is the disconnect between the condition and the promise; the second is the lack of assurance that the vow is heard despite the presence of the Spirit, as shown by Jephthah's condition that he will make an offering *if* victorious. Jephthah does not promise an appropriate offering related to his request and he does not trust in the Spirit. His vow is doomed and his daughter will pay the price.

## Human Sacrifice

If we assume that the laws of Leviticus applied to the period of the Judges, Leviticus 1–7 describes the gifts the Israelites were to bring to God. They were to be in the form of either animal or grain offerings. Acceptable animals included cattle, sheep, goats, doves, and pigeons. The animals must be male and unblemished. The blood of the animal was drained and smeared on the altar to designate the act as a sacrifice to God. Portions of the animal were burned as a gift to God. Other parts of the animal were given to the priests and their families as food. A complex series of laws designated specific sacrifices for various purposes. In general, sacrifices atoned for inadvertent sins that violated a commandment. Willful sins had to be atoned for by either ritual or punishment. In general, the purpose of sacrifice was to win God's favor.[8]

While animal sacrifice was an important part of Israelite worship, human sacrifice was considered an abomination before God.[9] Leviticus

---

[8] Sins against other people were to be handled directly by means of specified punishments. See W. Gunther Plaut, *The Torah: A Modern Commentary* (New York: Union of American Hebrew Congregations, 1981) 768; Susan Rattray, "Worship," *Harper's Bible Dictionary* 1143.

[9] For a more complete discussion of child sacrifice see Jon D. Levenson, *The Death and Resurrection of the Beloved Son* (New Haven: Yale University Press, 1993).

18:21 states: "You shall not give any of your offspring to sacrifice them to Molech [probably a Canaanite god], and so profane the name of your God: I am the LORD." The punishment for such a sacrifice was death by stoning (Lev 20:2-5). Furthermore, if anyone were to ignore an instance of human sacrifice, God would cut them off from among the people. During a reform King Josiah condemned Topheth in the Valley of Hinnom, where sons and daughters were said to "pass through fire" (2 Kgs 23:10). While some claim that "pass through fire" refers to a dedication of children to Molech, others contend that human sacrifice is intended. It seems more likely that the target of Josiah's reform was the practice of child sacrifice, as it would have been practiced by Canaanite neighbors, rather than a dedication ceremony. Jeremiah contends that Israelites offered up sons and daughters to Molech and that this was an abomination to God (Jer 32:25). Thus while human sacrifice is condemned, the biblical text indicates that Israelites practiced it.

Despite the injunction against human sacrifice, two Israelite kings were accused of making their sons "pass through fire." Ahaz "made his son pass through fire, according to the abominable practices of the nations" (2 Kgs 16:3). King Manasseh reinstated idol worship and "made his son pass through fire" (2 Kgs 21:6). The prophet Jeremiah issued an oracle of the LORD against this practice, reasserting that God never commanded human sacrifice (Jer 7:31).

The narrative most often used to illustrate that God does not desire human sacrifice is the testing of Abraham in Genesis 22. In this narrative God orders Abraham to take his son Isaac to Moriah and offer him to God as a burnt offering. Abraham obeys. Unlike the situation with Ahaz and Manasseh, Abraham does not perform this action within a context of returning to idolatrous practices, but as an act of obedience to God. Just as Abraham is about to kill Isaac, an angel of the LORD intervenes to stop the sacrifice. Human sacrifice is averted in accordance with the law in Leviticus and the oracle in Jeremiah.

In contrast to Genesis 22, Jephthah vows to offer a burnt offering of whatever or whoever comes out of his house first when he returns home. He receives no command from God to make a sacrifice, nor does he plan to use human sacrifice in a campaign to reinstate idolatry. There is no interruption by an angel telling him not to complete the sacrifice. Perhaps Jephthah's situation is more like that of the King of Moab, in which the trials of battle precipitate this extreme reaction (2 Kgs 3:27). Both Jephthah and the King of Moab fail to explore other alternatives in the heat of battle, but it is Jephthah's Israelite tradition that denounces the practice of human sacrifice.

## Women in Ancient Israel

Since there are no materials written by women in ancient Israel, we have no firsthand knowledge about women's lives in this period. What we have are collections of texts written by elite learned men from various time periods, including laws pertaining to women and narratives that include women as characters. However, we can gain impressions of women's lives and their role in Israelite society.

For the purpose of this work we assume the social scientific studies that analyze what lies behind the construction of biblical narratives about women. Sociology and anthropology have aided in the construction of a social framework for the period prior to the monarchy. Biblical narratives provide clues to power balances between men and women, but readers must take care not to superimpose current social categories, such as modern sex roles, upon the ancient world. Carol Meyers' findings are relevant here. She notes that there is less sexual stratification in a society when women make substantial contributions to the basic needs of the community, that is, when their roles are a major element in the productive labor of the community.[10] The three major areas of productivity are protection (military), production (food, shelter, and clothing), and procreation (child-bearing and child-rearing). According to Meyers, when women contribute as much as forty percent of the production effort, social stratification is less marked. It is obvious that tasks related to procreation were assigned to women and that most military activity was assigned to men. In Iron Age Palestine social stratification was less marked than in later periods. When portraying the role of women during pre-monarchical Israel we must also remember that the book of Judges reflects a variety of time periods beyond the period it purports to describe.

Since the family was the heart of the economic structure of Israel and family stories are featured in the Bible, historians can recover some information regarding the various roles women held in ancient Israel. Other sources that give clues to the role of women include archaeological discoveries of ancient settlements in and around Israel, as well as written and archaeological sources from surrounding cultures, such as Egypt and Mesopotamia. Archaeological discoveries are considered silent sources in that they yield artifacts, such as pottery, coins, or bone remains, all of which

---

[10] Carol L. Meyers, "Gender Roles and Genesis 3:16 Revisited," in Athalya Brenner, ed., *A Feminist Companion to Genesis* (Sheffield: Sheffield Academic Press, 1997) 122; Carol Meyers, *Rediscovering Eve: Ancient Israelite Women in Context* (New York: Oxford, 1988) 191.

then need interpretation. Written records can help interpret the artifacts. Comparative studies of other ancient cultures also provide clues about the world of women, which the Bible intentionally or unintentionally omits. The task of recovering information about women in ancient Israel is complex and ongoing.

Our attention will focus on what we might be able to surmise about women prior to the monarchy (1000 B.C.E.), when the economy was agrarian and based on growing crops and tending sheep and goats. Ideally scholars would like to make distinctions between time periods in Israelite history. However, given the nature of the editing process of the Tanakh, it is difficult to say a particular social structure is necessarily confined to a given period. Editors probably assumed that customs of their own day were practiced in an earlier period. Therefore the role of women in Israel after the monarchy could have found its way into accounts of earlier times. With this caution in mind, we will suggest a social milieu for early Israelite women.

Prior to the monarchy and the existence of cities, survival depended on the success of subsistence agriculture. The basic unit of the economy was the household, which consisted of a group of people related by either birth or marriage who depended on each other for economic survival.[11] Slaves were included within the household. Everyone contributed to the survival of the family unit. Women, men, and children carried out specific tasks, but each person's work was a necessary component of the success of the group. While the father was the head of the household, a more equal value was attached to the work of men and women than would be the case in later time periods. As a more urban society developed, the role of women, aside from childbearing and child rearing, was seen as less essential to the survival of the household. The status of women declined accordingly.

Ancient Israel traced its ancestors through a father-and-son line known as patrilineal descent. Men were the heads of households, and property was inherited through males.[12] Women were largely outsiders in the households of their husbands and sons. When a daughter married, she left her family home to reside in the home of her husband (Gen 24:4). A wife's duty was to produce children, preferably sons, and manage household tasks. The

---

[11] Naomi Steinberg, "Social Scientific Criticism: Judges 9 and Issues of Kinship," in Yee, ed., *Judges and Method,* 51.

[12] Phyllis Bird, "Women (OT)," *ABD* 6:952; Phyllis Bird, *Missing Persons and Mistaken Identities: Women and Gender in Ancient Israel* (Minneapolis: Fortress, 1997).

success of the family unit depended on producing offspring to perpetuate the economy of the household. Women spent much of their lives pregnant, and mortality rates were high for both children and mothers. If a woman died in childbirth, her husband generally took another wife.

A woman with sons had more security within her husband's family because sons were obliged to care for their parents in their old age (Exod 20:12). A woman without sons was at the mercy of her husband's family for support. Should she be banished from the family on account of barrenness, divorce, or upon her husband's death, she received no inheritance and had few alternatives.

The Torah records legislation meant to improve the plight of women. If a husband died it was the obligation of the dead husband's brother to marry the widow and impregnate her. Sons of that union were considered sons of the dead husband (Deut 25:5-10; Gen 38:1-30). This custom, known as levirate marriage, provided the widow with some security in her husband's family. Another piece of legislation allowed daughters to inherit land if they had no male siblings. The daughter was required to marry within the family of her father's clan so that the land did not pass from one tribe to another (Num 27:1-11; 36:5-9). If this legislation applied to the time period of the Judges, then when the daughter produced sons, the inheritance passed to the sons. In Judges 11 Jephthah has no sons, so the inheritance would presumably pass to his daughter and to her sons so long as she married within the tribe. With his daughter's death Jephthah's heritage is lost, and the land would revert to more distant male relatives, perhaps to his half-brothers who initially drove him out, saying that he would not inherit with them (Judg 11:1-4).

Within the household a mother was responsible for educating young children. Mothers instructed their sons and daughters in proper behavior. Children were expected to obey their parents (Exod 20:12). This obedience was meant to ensure the stability of the household.

At some point boys joined the men and were trained in the tasks of men, such as plowing, herding, and construction. Mothers raised their daughters in the skills necessary for being good wives within the households of their husbands. Food preparation skills included tending gardens, grinding grain, milking animals, and preserving and cooking foods. The making of clothing was a particularly time-consuming skill. Women prepared fibers, spun thread, wove cloth, and sewed garments. Tasks such as preparing hides and making pottery may have been shared with men.

The reference to Jephthah's daughter bewailing her virginity indicates that she intended to marry and fulfill the role expected of her as a daughter. Interestingly, Jephthah's wife or the mother of his daughter is not mentioned in Judges 11. First-century C.E. interpreters raise this question and imagine the existence of the daughter's mother and her sorrow at not being able to carry out wedding preparations for her daughter.[13]

Within the home women nursed the sick. Outside the immediate household they mourned the dead (Judg 11:40), functioned as midwives (Exod 1:15-22), mediums (1 Sam 28:3-7), prophets (Judg 4:4), and sages or wise women (2 Sam 14:4-7). Women also ministered at the entrance of the tent of meeting (Exod 38:8). These more independent roles were most likely reserved for women past childbearing age. Of these more public roles, the one most relevant to Judg 11:29-40 is that of a mourning woman. Judges 11:40 states that the daughters of Israel continued to lament the daughter of Jephthah for four days each year. The Bible makes no further mention of this particular tradition, but there is evidence in the Bible and in other ancient Near Eastern texts that women functioned as mourners of the dead. As mourners, women washed and anointed bodies in preparation for burial. They also engaged in public weeping and intoned laments. Other signs of mourning included wearing sackcloth, tearing clothing, accompanying the body to the gravesite, and returning at regular intervals to the gravesite to mourn the dead.[14] Evidence for women mourners is found in Jer 9:17:

> Thus says the LORD of hosts: Consider, and call for the mourning women to come; send for the skilled women to come; let them quickly raise a dirge over us, so that our eyes may run down with tears, and our eyelids flow with water.

It is apparent that women also trained their daughters in the art of lamenting the dead (Jer 9:20). The women who mourned the daughter of Jephthah in Judg 11:40 might have included women skilled in the art of keening laments and in the composition of laments. Cross-cultural studies show that there were set categories of laments, but that laments were also improvised to speak of the specific individual mourned.[15] Since there is no record

---

[13] Pseudo-Philo, in James H. Charlesworth, ed., *The Old Testament Pseudepigrapha* (Garden City, NY: Doubleday, 1985) 353.

[14] For a more detailed study of women mourners see Barbara B. Miller, *Women, Death, and Mourning in the Ancient Eastern Mediterranean World* (University of Michigan, Ann Arbor, MI: University Microfilms International, 1994). For women's participation in funeral processions during the medieval period see Rachel S. Hallote, *Death, Burial, and Afterlife in the Biblical World* (Chicago: Ivan R. Dee, 2001) 162.

[15] Ibid. 290.

of a specific lament attributed to the daughters of Israel, it will be the task of later interpreters, early rabbis, and modern interpreters to fill in this narrative gap.

A daughter's sexuality was under the control of her father until marriage and then under the control of her husband. This is evident in Deut 22:13-21, where a newly married husband claims that his wife was not a virgin *(betulah)* at first intercourse. The father and mother of the daughter were obliged to produce the tokens of the daughter's virginity, namely a cloth bearing blood indicating that the young woman's hymen was broken during first intercourse. If the cloth containing blood was produced, the husband had to pay a fine to the father and was not allowed to divorce his wife. If the bloody cloth was not produced, the men of the town could stone the woman to death. The point here is that physical virginity *(betulah)* was expected of a bride.

The same term, *betulah,* translated "virginity" in the *NRSV,* is used in Judg 11:37-38 when the daughter requests to go to the mountains for two months to bewail her virginity. In this reference *betulah* indicates a broader category of women, most likely young women who have reached puberty and can bear a child. This use of the term is discussed more fully in Chapter Five.

Further indication of how a daughter's sexuality was guarded by either her father or husband is found in the adultery and rape laws in Deut 22:23-29. These laws make a distinction between a married woman, an engaged woman, and a woman who is not engaged. If a man has sex with a married woman both are to die. In this case the wronged party is the woman's husband because his property has been violated. If an engaged woman has sex with a man in a town, both are to die because it is assumed that if it was rape, the woman would have cried out and been heard. If this happened in the country no one would have heard her and only the man was to be punished by death. If the woman was a virgin (probably nubile, hence marriageable) but not engaged, the man had to pay a fine to her father (the wronged party) and marry her without possibility of divorce. In Judg 11:39, when Jephthah's daughter returns from the mountains the narrator says that she never slept with a man. This statement rules out any suspicion that she had sex during her two months away. The *betulah* or nubile daughter is "unblemished" and thus a fitting sacrifice.

If Jephthah's daughter had lived to be married, her marriage would have consisted of two steps. The first was an engagement or betrothal in which the parents of the bride and groom agreed on a "bride price." The groom's family paid the "bride price" to the bride's family. Other gifts might also be given. For example, when Abraham's servant negotiates with

Rebekah's family he offers lavish gifts to Rebekah, her brother, and her mother (Gen 24:52-53). Interestingly, Rebekah is given the choice as to whether she wants to enter the marriage. The second step was the home-taking, when the bride left her family and went to live with the groom's family.[16] In Rebekah's case she leaves immediately after the exchange of gifts. A celebration might accompany the home-taking (Gen 29:21-23). Speculation concerning Jephthah's daughter's wedding is found in the midrash *Pseudo-Philo* 40 discussed in Chapter Four.

## A Literary Approach to the Bible

Discussion of historical, political, social, and religious circumstances that lie behind biblical texts is important. However, this is not the main reason many people read and honor the Bible. As sacred text, the Bible testifies to a wide range of human experience that transcends modern notions of historical veracity. There is no historical proof that Jephthah made a vow and as a result sacrificed his daughter, yet the power of the narrative stirs the reader to wonder, for example, what kind of man Jephthah was and what kind of God mandated the keeping of vows. Every generation of readers knows about fathers who are shortsighted, who abuse daughters, and who foment national tragedy. Every generation asks how such things can happen, where God is, and where hope can be found. Biblical narratives allow readers past and present to reflect on the human condition in light of their faith in God.

Modern literary criticism addresses these concerns through a synchronic (same time) approach to biblical narrative that accepts the text as it is presented, without much attention to historical matters. For example, literary criticism studies the meanings of words in a text, their arrangement (syntax), the text's themes, and literary forms. It is concerned with setting, characters, plot, and the development and resolution of tension within the narrative. The literary critic analyzes the point of view of the narrator and possible messages the narrative conveys.

### The Nature of Biblical Narrative

Many scholars suppose that biblical narratives originated as stories that were transmitted orally from generation to generation in various social

---

[16] An exception to the custom of patrilocal marriage is Jacob's marriage to Leah and Rachel, after which he remains in Laban's household, in Genesis 29.

settings over hundreds of years, or perhaps only a few years, before they were written down. Oral tradition implies that stories are continually adapted to different audiences over time. Likewise, storytellers wishing to highlight themes in a given narrative might change the story to fit the storyteller's point of view. Thus in its inception and transmission oral tradition is fluid.

Once oral tradition attains written form, biblical redactors (editors) impose literary constraints on narratives. A story that was told perhaps during a long starlit night around a campfire is altered to fit written form. The narrative may be shortened, as is evident in the economy of biblical stories. Literary critics note numerous literary strategies in these narratives. Three examples will be noted here. First, narratives frequently exhibit plays on words or puns that enliven oral storytelling or reading of the text in Hebrew. For example, the Hebrew root ʿbr occurs three times in Judg 11:29-30. The *NRSV* indicates that Jephthah passed through *(ʿbr)* Gilead and Manasseh, ʿbr Mizpah, and ʿbr on to the Ammonites. Robert Boling translates the final occurrence of ʿbr as "stalked," indicating that Jephthah's purpose is to make war rather than to merely "pass through" the land.[17] Second, a repetition of words or phrases that was so necessary for hearers of the story is undoubtedly decreased in the economy of the written text. Such repetition is found in Judges 11 in phrases such as "opened my/your mouth" and "bewail my virginity." Repetition of these phrases stresses important thematic issues such as keeping a vow and the tragedy of a woman dying prior to bearing children. Third, in the process of editing, certain elements of the story may be reconfigured to reflect a more universal theological stance. In the Jephthah narrative one could interpret God's absence in the text as either an indication that the keeping of a vow at all costs needs no interpretation or refinement or that the human community itself is responsible for the refinement of such teachings.

It is obvious that we have no access to oral versions of biblical narratives. We have no manuscript editions of the narratives prior to those found among the Dead Sea Scrolls at Qumran. These biblical manuscripts, some of which date to the second century B.C.E., provide our earliest known manuscripts of the Bible. In taking a literary approach to Judges 11 we must acknowledge that there are wide gaps in what we can know about the origin and transmission of the biblical story.

Literary critics identify other characteristics of biblical narratives in addition to the ones illustrated above. For example, at times biblical stories

---

[17] Boling, *Judges,* 207.

contain non sequiturs or details not pertinent to the story at hand.[18] In Gen 22:20-24 a genealogy of Abraham's kin follows the near sacrifice of Abraham's son Isaac. The significance of this information only unfolds later in Isaac's marriage to Rebekah. Second, certain narrative motifs are repeated in similar stories in which characters or place names are altered. A wife/sister motif is repeated in three narratives (Gen 12:10-20; 20:1-18; 26:1-16). Third, themes such as sibling rivalry are repeated in numerous stories, as in the narratives of Jacob and Esau and Leah and Rachel. Fourth, etiologies attempt to explain place names, personal name changes, or the origin of customs. Judges 11:40 mentions a tradition in which the daughters of Israel annually mourn the daughter of Jephthah. Fifth, integral to some biblical narratives is a symmetrical pattern of words within a verse or thematic ideas in an entire narrative. Thematic symmetry will be illustrated in Chapter Four.

Thus far, we have relied on scholars proficient in the study of literary matters to illustrate various aspects of biblical narrative. They have used a wide variety of approaches and applied them to a myriad of biblical texts in scholarly journals and books. As students of the Bible we could just imitate one of these methods and apply it to the Jephthah text. However, I suggest a more creative technique to enhance our literary analysis and prepare us not only to appreciate medieval midrash, but also to create our own modern midrash. In this next section I will describe this technique for close reading of biblical narratives and illustrate it with examples from the story of Jephthah's daughter.

## A Technique for Close Reading of a Narrative

In general, the close reading technique consists of four steps. In step one the reader uses color coding to distinguish characters, actions performed by characters, literary aspects, such as repetition and thematic symmetry, and an identification of major themes. Step two highlights the elements of the plot, namely the narrative exposition, complication, change, unraveling, and ending. Step three focuses on the point of view of the narrator as well as that of major and minor characters. This step relies only on information stated in the narrative and provides an opportunity to note values the narrator brings to the text. Finally, the fourth step identifies narrative silences by finding gaps in the storyline. How did the story get from one point to another? How can these gaps serve as points for creating midrash?

---

[18] Joel Rosenberg, "Bible: Biblical Narrative," in Barry W. Holtz, ed., *Back to the Sources: Reading the Classic Jewish Texts* (New York: Summit Books, 1984) 37.

*Step One:*
*Developing an Organizing Thesis Through Color Coding*

The following technique for close reading of a text was developed by David McCarthy.[19] The first strategy in color coding is to become intimately familiar with a text so that its literary quality is revealed to the reader. According to McCarthy it is necessary to read the text "seventy times," so that one begins to experience the text for oneself. Avoid the temptation to consult commentaries, because they tend to reflect someone else's experience of the text. The process of close reading affirms the reader's ability to interact with the text without the influence of scholars or theologians.

The second strategy is to reproduce the text on a computer screen so it is possible to see the relationships of the smaller units to the text as a whole as well as allowing color coding of the copy. It is best to use an English version of the Bible that reflects a scholarly translation from the original Hebrew text. The *New Revised Standard Version* is recommended.

To color-code a text, assign a particular color to various significant patterns within a particular text. For example, the various names for the deity, such as God or LORD or angel of the LORD, can be underlined in red. A further distinction can be made by circling "God" in red, underlining "LORD" in red and placing a red box around "angel of the LORD." Such distinctions not only reveal the author's preference for naming the deity but also show how the deity communicates with humans. Does the deity speak directly or through an intermediary, such as a messenger or angel? Other characters in the narrative can be noted by different colors—Jephthah and pronouns referring to him in orange, the daughter in green, and the companions in purple. Relationships between characters can be noted by highlighting the familial language in the text. The repeated use of "daughter" in Judges 11 indicates that, as far as the text is concerned, she has no name and is identified by her relationship with her father.

Once all the characters are identified, color code the verbs and list the verbs associated with each character. Make a distinction between active and passive verbs. Who performs actions and who are the objects of actions? Is one character more active and another more passive? Note the tenses of verbs. Since we are using an English translation, the verb analysis will rely on English tenses, although the verb tenses convey different meanings in

[19] My thanks to David McCarthy for sharing his unpublished manuscript, *Reading the Bible Close Up and Personal,* and for permitting me to use his close reading technique with my classes at Edgewood College.

Hebrew. Who speaks in the imperative and what type of authority does the character exhibit? According to McCarthy there is no limit to the number of categories for color coding. One might note words used for emphasis, intensifiers, metaphors, words used in parallel, place names, repeating words, time words, and attention-getting devices. It is important, however, to limit the number of patterns one focuses on in a given text; categories that do not yield information leading to a significant thesis or theme should be eliminated.

The third strategy is to discover what significant patterns exist in the text and how they function. Arrange similarly color-coded items in categories reflecting themes conveyed in the text. For example, both Jephthah and the LORD are named. The unnamed character, identified only in relation to her father, is the one who is sacrificed. This pattern might indicate that not having a name implies expendability. Experiment with various patterns until a workable one emerges.

The observation that such a pivotal character in the narrative is left nameless and identified only by her relationship to a man leads to strategy four. This is what McCarthy calls a "wow moment," in which an organizing thesis reveals itself. An organizing thesis for Judges 11 might be: a named father holds life-and-death power over his unnamed daughter. Such a statement shocks both ancient and modern sensibilities, begging for a closer reading of the text. This thesis raises questions about how the text has been interpreted in the past and whether that interpretation has value for today.

Let us apply some of these strategies to the actions of the characters in Judg 11:29-40. Active verbs associated with Jephthah indicate that he passes through various towns, makes a vow saying what he will do when he returns home victorious, and fights the Ammonites. He inflicts a massive defeat upon them. He comes home, sees his daughter, and tears his clothes in despair. He speaks to her of his dilemma. He refuses to take back his vow. He sends his daughter away for two months; then, upon her return, he does with her according to his vow. Passive verbs indicate that Jephthah receives the Spirit of the LORD and victory over the Ammonites, actions attributed to God. Both actions imply that God was in control of the battle. Jephthah's direct action of making a vow intrudes into God's action. Jephthah's actions after the vow are mostly violent: he inflicts defeat, he blames his daughter by telling her that she has brought him very low, he sends her away, and ultimately he carries out his vow. It should also be noted that in tearing his clothes, a sign of mourning, Jephthah grieves the turn of events.

Thesis formation is, by nature, open-ended and considerably subjective. The thesis comes partially from the word groups chosen for color coding and also from the creativity of the investigator. The choice of a thesis is not to be taken lightly; it must resonate with the text and with the goals of the investigator.

The actions attributed to Jephthah's daughter include greeting her father, dancing, affirming her father's vow, agreeing to be a sacrifice, acknowledging that the military victory is more important than her life, requesting a two-month respite, bewailing her virginity twice, departing to the mountains, returning, and never sleeping with a man. The progression of these actions can be matched with appropriate emotional responses. She is joyful in greeting her father, acquiescent to his plight, sad at not being able to fulfill her life, and accepting of her fate. Emotionally she progresses from joy to an acceptance of her own death. As a young woman she moves from naïvete to harsh reality. If we compare Jephthah's actions with the daughter's actions we note that, once he returns home, his behavior controls her. Her only attempt to assert control is requesting time away with her friends. An organizing thesis might be that a daughter has little or no autonomy to manage her own life.

In the five times that the LORD is mentioned in Judg 11:29-40, only two actions are attributed to the deity. The LORD sends the Spirit to Jephthah, and the LORD delivers the Ammonites into Jephthah's hands. Passively, the LORD is the one to whom vows and sacrifices are made. In this narrative God becomes involved with Israel's military security by inspiring a leader and by delivering up the enemy. Neither of these activities relates to Jephthah's daughter. Jephthah's vow and sacrifice are Jephthah's doing. After the battle the LORD withdraws from the action of the narrative altogether. Might an organizing thesis be that God is not involved in the minute events of human life, or is it that humans are responsible for the consequences of their actions?

This technique for becoming familiar with a text and drawing a thesis out of it is one means of interpreting a text. The questions raised by this technique may not be answered by traditional theologies. They may be unsettling and push us to investigate new interpretations. Hence the Bible does not directly answer the deep quandaries of human existence, but it provides endless opportunities for reflection.

*Step Two:*
*Determining the Plot*

Literary study of biblical narrative analyzes the elements related to plot development. This involves the exposition (beginning) and conclusion of the narrative and the intervening development of the plot, including its setting, the development of tension or complication, a pivot or change point, and a resolution of tension or unraveling of the narrative.[20]

A particular biblical narrative is marked by a beginning and an end. The stage is set for the story of Jephthah by recounting his parentage, his ouster from his family, his summoning to return as a military leader, and his vow. His story concludes with the sacrifice of his daughter, the intertribal warfare against Ephraim and, finally, his death (Judg 12:7). The markers of birth and death are natural boundaries of the narrative.

Narratives are arranged in chronological order, especially when the text purports to be historical. The battle with the Ammonites and the place names serve to establish Jephthah within a "history" of the pre-monarchical period. As noted above, modern historians encounter numerous problems when attempting to create a history of ancient Israel.

Within Jephthah's larger story we can identify the portion of the narrative related to Jephthah's daughter, marked by the elements that frame her life and death: namely the descent of the Spirit of the LORD upon her father prior to battle, Jephthah's vow and her consent to the vow, and her tragic death (Judg 11:29-40). One might argue that the daughter's story begins with her first appearance when she comes out of the house to greet her father. However, a framework that includes Jephthah's vow explains the complication or development of tension in the narrative. Jephthah's reception of the Spirit of the LORD adds a further complication by involving God's presence as a backdrop to Jephthah's vow.

The beginning or exposition of the daughter's narrative (Judg 11:29) establishes the presence of the Spirit of the LORD which comes upon Jephthah prior to his searching out the Ammonites. All seems well when Jephthah receives the Spirit and victory seems assured. Complication (Judg 11:30-33) enters the narrative when Jephthah makes a vow to sacrifice whatever or whoever comes out from his house upon his return. The change in the narrative (Judg 11:34) occurs when his daughter is the first to greet him on his return. Tension grips the reader in anticipation of a resolution. What are the possibilities of resolution? The rest of the story (Judg 11:35-39) involves the unraveling of events: the confrontation between father and daughter, her request for a delay, her time on the mountain, her return, and her death. The plot ends with the women commemorating her death (Judg 11:40).

On the surface the progression from one element of the plot to another produces a coherent story. However, within each element we can identify gaps in the story. This is particularly true in the unraveling section. Here

---

[20] Yairah Amit, *Reading Biblical Narrative: Literary Criticism and the Hebrew Bible* (Minneapolis: Fortress, 2001) 46.

we can identify various scenes. The first occurs at Jephthah's home and contains the conversation with his daughter and her departure. The second scene is much abbreviated, stating that she and her companions bewailed her virginity on the mountains. The third scene is even more abbreviated, noting that she returned home and her father carried out his vow. Following this mapping of the plot, we are able to identify narrative gaps as locations for creating midrash, as described in strategy four.

*Step Three:*
*The Point of View of the Narrator*

The narrator of a biblical story is one who directs the plot, setting, and characters of the narrative. The story is in the writer's hands. The creator of the story controls the characters, including the role God plays in the narrative, and is responsible for portraying God in keeping with the belief system of ancient Israel. According to Yairah Amit, the narrator and the portrayal of God should always be believable for the reader.[21] The narrator is also responsible for portraying a particular point of view. It may be an overt point of view as in 2 Sam 12:24 when Bathsheba gives birth to Solomon, the next king of Israel, and the narrator comments: "The LORD loved him." In Judg 11:29 the Spirit of the LORD comes upon Jephthah. In these examples the narrator affirms that both men are guided by God and will succeed. On other occasions the point of view may be more subtle. In Judges 11 the narrator does not overtly judge Jephthah's action in carrying out his vow, but does state that Jephthah ruled for only six years, as opposed to the twenty or forty years allotted to some of the other judges.

One way of discerning the narrator's point of view is to retell the story from the viewpoint of various characters. To try this technique, choose a character from the Jephthah narrative and retell the story from that perspective in either the first or third person. Do not attribute motives to the character that are not mentioned in the story. Use only the details given. The resulting retelling will most likely seem abrupt and incomplete, thus highlighting the role of the narrator.

The characters in Judg 11:29-40 include the Spirit of the LORD, the LORD, Jephthah, the Ammonites, Jephthah's daughter, the daughter's companions, and the daughters of Israel. For example, if Jephthah's daughter were telling the story it might be: "I greeted my victorious father with timbrels and dancing. His response was to tear his clothes and grieve that I was the cause of deep trouble to him on account of a vow that he made to

---
[21] Ibid. 101.

the LORD. I told him that he must keep his vow since the LORD had given him victory. I requested a two-month sojourn in the mountains with my companions to bewail my virginity. After the two months I returned to my father, who carried out his vow." In this retelling Jephthah's daughter is quick to uphold her father's vow without debate, requesting only a two-month respite with friends. She is obedient to what is assumed to be an ethic of unbreakable vows. It appears that the narrator supports this agenda as well—children must be obedient to their parents, especially when an obligation to the LORD is involved.

Jephthah's version of the story might sound like this: "The Spirit of the LORD came upon me as I was going into battle. I made a vow to the LORD that I would offer as a burnt offering whoever/whatever came out of my house upon my victorious return. Alas, it was my daughter. I tore my clothes and blamed her. She understood my dilemma and asked for a time with her friends. I granted this but, in the end, fulfilled the vow." This retelling of the narrative is close to the voice of the narrator. The narrator does add a few details about the daughter's never sleeping with a man and the annual lament over the daughter to enhance the theme and the sadness of the story.

The daughter's companions come into the story late. They might give the following version of the story: "We accompanied Jephthah's daughter to the mountains, where we joined her in bewailing her virginity or her childless state. After our two-month stay she returned to her father." This retelling emphasizes a communal response to the daughter's not being able to fulfill her role as a mother. The narrator then adds the detail that she never slept with a man prior to being sacrificed, emphasizing her tragically unfulfilled life.

The LORD's version of the story might be stated this way: "I sent my spirit upon Jephthah prior to battle. He then invoked a vow in my name. Both Jephthah and his daughter recognized the validity of the vow because it was connected with Jephthah's success in battle." In this retelling, the most active engagement the LORD has in the narrative is to be the conveyer of the spirit. Otherwise, the narrative is out of the hands of the LORD, who essentially withdraws from the narrative. The human characters are left to work out a resolution. It appears that the narrator removes the LORD from the scene to enhance the human tragedy that follows.

By using this technique of presenting multiple points of view one can distinguish the narrator's point of view. The narrator's message is that the LORD gives the spirit, but humans fail to see its potential. They take matters into their own hands, and tragedy results. This message is a common theme throughout the Tanakh. Reading the narrative from the point of view of other characters, using only the details presented, sets the stage for recognizing where narrative silences occur.

## *Step Four:*
## *Reading for Narrative Silences*

We will now examine what the text does not say and what themes are left unresolved by the narrator. While the point-of-view exercise highlights the narrator's main theme, we are left with gaps in the text. We are aware of missing emotions, motivations, and details that might enhance an understanding of the narrative. Some of the narrative silences in Judg 11:29-40 include Jephthah's motivation for making the vow, whether or not the daughter knew of her father's victory prior to his return, the absence of a mother, and any conversation prior to the daughter's reply: "do to me according to what has gone out of your mouth." Also missing are the activity on the mountain, the actual description of her death, and the content of the ceremony celebrated by the daughters of Israel for four days each year.

For example, if Jephthah's daughter had had a more extended conversation with her father before she consented to his carrying out his vow she might have explored other options with him. What were the laws regarding vows? Were there alternatives? Were there authorities to consult regarding this dilemma? Were there legal loopholes that could be invoked? As the narrative stands, none of these options is explored. Jewish scholars filled in these gaps with midrash, i.e., new stories based on the text and relevant to issues in their own day. These midrashim often specified a legal point or social dilemma alluded to in the story. Through the process of creating and discussing a particular midrash the scholars were able to develop an active dialogue with the text.

In addition to raising legal and social issues, narrative silences push us to contemplate God's place in the narrative.[22] In her analysis of Ehud, the Israelite deliverer in Judg 3:12-30, Yairah Amit claims that narrative gaps suggest to her that someone, namely God, has taken care of the details. Therefore it is legitimate to move from event to event in the narrative without undue concern for the silences. If this were the case in Judg 11:29-40, it would appear that the Spirit of the LORD coming upon Jephthah, the vow, the daughter's acquiescence, and the carrying out of the vow are all in accord with God's plan. Such an interpretation has God agreeing with child sacrifice. The prophet Jeremiah, medieval interpreters, and modern readers

---

[22] Ibid. 61.

find this portrayal of God appalling. The issue here is whether God micro-manages human affairs or allows humans the freedom to act within a set of moral guidelines. This question goes to the very nature of the relationship between God and human beings. Medieval midrash may be creative, even to the point of being fanciful, but it still operates within boundaries. Midrash maintains the existence of a monotheistic God who sets limits for behavior and grants humans freedom to live responsibly within those limits.

## Looking Ahead

In this chapter we have provided a brief overview of historical-social issues important to understanding the narrative of Jephthah's daughter, as well as a discussion of the elements of biblical narrative. The text relies on an appreciation of the significance of the Spirit of the LORD, the making and keeping of vows, the existence and condemnation of the practice of human sacrifice, and the role of women in ancient Israel. In the following chapters we will create a dialogue in which we, as modern readers, join medieval rabbis and feminist interpreters in a discussion of the tragic story of Jephthah's daughter. The portrait of women presented in Chapter One forms a basis for the feminist interpretation found in Chapters Three and Five. Our literary analysis of the elements of a narrative—specifically plot, point of view, and the recognition of narrative content and silences—forms a basis in Chapters Two and Four for appreciating the medieval Jewish midrash.

# CHAPTER TWO

*Rabbinic Midrash as a Conversation Partner*

One of our partners in the conversation about Jephthah's daughter is a group of Jewish rabbis (scholars) who lived during the medieval period. They offer us continuity between past and present through their interpretation of the sacred texts. In this chapter we will trace the development of their work and illustrate their techniques with examples from their writings. We will focus on the literary form of midrash after a brief survey of the other forms of rabbinic interpretation.

Historically, the contents of the Tanakh were authoritatively fixed roughly near the end of the first century C.E., but the text has been kept alive as generation after generation has applied it to community life in ethics, law, and literature. This body of interpretation is found in a variety of forms, namely legal debate in the Mishnah, expansion of legal debate through narrative illustration in the Talmud, and legend or folklore collections called midrash. We will trace the development of each of these writings.

The ongoing interpretation of the Bible is evident in the Scripture itself. Nehemiah 8:1-12 speaks of an incident in which the book of the law (Torah) was first read and interpreted. After the return from exile in Babylon (ca. 450 B.C.E.) the scribe Ezra read from the book of the law to the people gathered at the Water Gate in Jerusalem. They all stood up when he read from the book, and when Ezra blessed God, the people replied, "Amen." The reading continued from early morning to midday as the Levites (temple officials) moved about the crowd offering interpretation of the book. "They gave the sense, so that the people understood the reading" (Neh 8:8). On this occasion the "sense" probably meant that the Levites translated the book, which was written in Hebrew, into Aramaic, the spoken language of the listeners. After this period, interpretation is not limited to translation issues, but entails updating the biblical text to conform to different historical contexts.

Scholarly commentaries are a quick way to research basic questions related to interpreting a particular biblical passage. Modern commentaries typically present the text in a commonly accepted translation or one offered by the author. The author's comments may concern linguistic, archaeological, historical, or literary issues. The writer usually compares the given text to related texts in the Bible or other Near Eastern texts. Some commentaries are written to highlight particular sociological themes, such as human oppression, as found in liberationist, feminist, and other interpretations. Many commentaries update information from older commentaries, often summarizing the discussion that has occurred over the years about a particular passage. For the most part these commentaries do not consider values or encourage a faith response.

Another type of commentary is that written expressly as a guide for sermon preparation, aimed at promoting certain themes within faith communities. A theme in a particular text is highlighted and compared to the same theme in other biblical texts. The theme then is related to an issue in today's world. For example, the description of the creation of the world in Genesis 1 and various texts discussing the beauty of creation in the Psalms might provide biblical support for a sermon calling for environmental responsibility. The purpose of rabbinic commentary is much like that of these sermon-writing commentaries, although, as we will see, they differ in style.

## Ancient Rabbinic Commentary: The Mishnah

Written rabbinic commentaries, as early as 200 B.C.E., are similar to modern commentaries in that they begin with a passage from the Torah that requires elaboration. The Torah contains six hundred thirteen laws (teachings) considered binding on Jews. Problems arose, however, because, as Israel was repeatedly conquered and dispersed throughout the Middle East, the laws did not relate to the circumstances of the people. Take, for example, the commandment against murdering another human being. "You shall not kill" did not differentiate as to whether a killing involved self-defense, war, or homicide. Controversies over issues of law were brought before the judges—priests, elders, scribes, or rabbis—and were decided by majority rule. Over time the judgments rendered in these cases became known as the Oral Law. Rabbi Judah haNasi is credited with compiling the Oral Law, comprising hundreds of judicial opinions noting both majority and minority opinions, into a written form known as the Mishnah. The Mishnah records disagreements among the rabbis. No decisive conclusion is reached for the various cases. The arguments presented most often raise further questions, thereby leaving room for subsequent interpretation.[1]

Since Torah laws were considered binding, some laws required extensive interpretation. For example, the Torah cites a case involving a rebellious son. In this situation the father and mother are to take the son to the elders of the town and declare, "This son of ours is stubborn and rebellious. He will not obey us. He is a glutton and a drunkard." The men of the town are to stone the son to death (Deut 21:18-21). Harry Gersh claims that, while this law might have made sense during a time of ancient warfare, it later became outmoded.[2] Since the law had to stand, various interpretations specified the age of the son, the definition of gluttony and drunkenness, and other details. In the end the Oral Law (Mishnah) said that the youth had to be over age thirteen. (In practice a young man would not be required to obey his parents after he turned thirteen because he would be considered a man.) Gluttony was defined as eating a pound of meat at one sitting. Drunkenness consisted of drinking a pint of wine at one sitting without eating food. If wine was consumed with food or during a festival, it was not considered drunkenness. Obviously it would be very difficult to meet the criteria for the stoning to be carried out. The law stands, yet it is protected by conditions that mitigate harsh punishment for the accused.

Mishnaic commentary focuses on legal material in the Torah. The form of the commentary is to address specific Torah precedents as they apply to ongoing social and legal changes. Many of the laws in the Mishnah were no longer relevant when they took written form; therefore the purpose of the Mishnah was to serve not so much as a code of conduct but as an example of legal debate as applied to life in the Jewish community.

## Medieval Commentary:
## The Talmud

Subsequent developments in rabbinic interpretation, like the Mishnah, were also mainly legal in nature. In the centuries following the writing of the Mishnah, debate continued, new cases emerged, and refinements of laws were made. The Gemara, a second body of interpretation of the law, was added to the Mishnah to form the Talmud. Actually two versions of the

---

[1] Robert Goldenberg, "Talmud," in Barry W. Holtz, ed., *Back to the Sources: Reading the Classic Jewish Texts* (New York: Summit Books, 1984) 134.

[2] Harry Gersh, *Mishnah: The Oral Law* (West Orange, NJ: Behrman House, 1984) 7.

Talmud developed. The Jerusalem Talmud was completed by 400 C.E. and the Babylonian Talmud by 500 C.E. Of the two, the Babylonian Talmud became the object of intensive study and the more authoritative source. The Talmud itself was reinterpreted by Rashi in the eleventh century and then again by scholars following him. Today each page of the Talmud contains a Mishnah text, the Gemara related to the Mishnah text, commentary by Rashi, and various commentaries by other scholars. For Jews the Talmud contains the wisdom and ethics of their tradition and continues to be open to interpretation.

To illustrate the relationship between the Torah, the Mishnah, and the Talmud, we will trace tradition regarding the making and annulment of vows in all three. In Chapter One we considered vows in the Torah when we compared Jephthah's vow with three other biblical vows. That comparison was literary in nature; here we will examine the legal status of a vow in Jewish tradition as it develops.

A vow was a promise made to God to perform a deed or to abstain from something that was normally permitted.[3] Laws concerning vows state that when a man makes a vow to the LORD he is not to break his word (Num 30:2). When a woman makes a vow to the LORD it can be nullified by either her father or her husband, depending on which has authority over her. In either case the father or husband must nullify the vow when he first hears of it. The woman is then forgiven the vow (Num 30:3-16). According to Deut 23:21-22 the maker of a vow is obliged to fulfill the vow without delay once it is made. This passage emphasizes the need to fulfill a vow but cautions that one needs to be careful about making a vow. If one refrains from making a vow, no guilt will result. It might be better not to make one at all. The writer of Ecclesiastes repeats this advice, saying that it is better not to make a vow lest God regard you as a fool or destroy your work (Eccl 5:4-6).

The tractate (section) in the Mishnah, entitled *Nedarim* or "vows," concerns vows that are not binding on an individual, limitations placed on vows, and releasing a person from a vow. (It appears that vows were made frequently in the early centuries of the Common Era, and the rabbis were concerned with their proliferation.) The following entry illustrates the nature of a Mishnah dialogue. Entry A states the issue to be discussed. The subsequent entries list related opinions of other rabbis. One opinion may contradict another.

---

[3] Louis Isaac Rabinowitz, "Vows and Vowing," *Encyclopaedia Judaica* (Jerusalem: Kater Publishing, 1972) 227.

A. He who vows not to have milk is permitted to eat curds.

B. And R. Yose prohibits eating curds.

C. If he vowed not to eat curds, he is permitted to have milk.

D. Abba Saul says, "He who vows not to eat cheese is prohibited to eat it whether it is salted or unsalted. *m. Ned.* 6:5.[4]

In this example there is a disagreement over whether one can eat curds (a milk product) if one takes a vow not to drink milk. The comment by Abba Saul, regarding eating salted or unsalted cheese, is included among the opinions about milk and curds, but it could be a separate issue depending on whether one considers curds to be cheese. Note that there is no final resolution to the issue, only a variety of related or loosely related opinions. The rest of this tractate concerns vows made by women and the more detailed circumstances under which they could be annulled.

In the Babylonian Talmud the tractate *Nedarim* (vows) expands the previous discussion. It reproduces the Mishnah tractate *Nedarim,* adding more commentary or opinions by other rabbis. This added commentary is called the Gemara.[5] In the discussion about making a vow not to drink milk, the Gemara clarifies the relationship between milk and other related foods. A person who vows not to drink milk is permitted curds. A person who refrains from curds is permitted milk. A person who refrains from milk is permitted cheese. And a person who refrains from cheese is permitted milk (*b. Ned.* 52b). The Gemara separates each of these foods so as to prevent the vow from becoming too broad. Interpreting the vow too broadly could result in someone eliminating too many foods from the diet. In cultures where food supplies were limited, an overzealous prohibition of available foods could endanger an individual's health, the well-being of the family, and even the welfare of the wider community.

Vowing not to eat a particular food may seem to be a minor issue and not worthy of all the attention given it in the Mishnah and Talmud, but it illustrates the larger picture regarding the making and keeping of vows. All of this attention indicates that making vows had gotten out of hand. People were either making vows they were not able to keep or they were making vows that had negative implications for the community at large. Those who did not take into consideration all the ramifications of the vow might later

---

[4] *The Mishnah: A New Translation,* trans. Jacob Neusner (New Haven: Yale University Press, 1988) 417.

[5] *The Babylonian Talmud: Seder Nashim* 5, trans. Harry Freedman, ed. Isidore Epstein (London: Soncino, 1936).

wish they had not made the vow in the first place. There is provision for annulling a vow in the Talmud. The annulment was to take place before three men who could render the vow null with the words: "It is absolved to you, it is absolved to you" (*b. Sanh.* 68a).[6] However, this procedure was limited to a small category of vows.

The majority opinion in the Talmud is that one should not make vows in the first place. The overriding principle is that "whatever your lips utter you must diligently perform" (Deut 23:23). One's word is one's word without the necessity of a vow. One rabbi goes so far as to say that to make a vow is like building a high place (a rival shrine to the Temple in Jerusalem) and to keep the vow is like making a sacrifice on it (*Nedarim* 22a). While this statement is extreme compared to other opinions in the Talmud, it reiterates the advice against vows. Value is found in truth telling, not oath taking. Rabbi ben Judah said, "Let your yes be yes, your no be no."[7]

What does this discussion about vows have to do with Jephthah's vow? It would seem that a vow about not eating milk or cheese is not on the same level as a vow to offer who/whatever first comes forth from one's house as a burnt offering. However, the point is that the vows are valid in that they both invoke God's name in a promise. When Jephthah made his vow he did not foresee its implications. Tragedy could have been averted if he had not acted so rashly. We wonder if any mechanisms were in place for Jephthah to have his vow annulled. The Bible does not specify a procedure for this, but the issue is raised by later sages in the form of midrash. Midrash suggests that Jephthah could have gone to Phinehas, a priest, for consultation, but that is not part of the biblical story. The Phinehas solution to Jephthah's plight probably reflects a procedure already in place by the fourth century when the midrash was written. The talmudic tractate *Nedarim* does not mention Jephthah in its discussion about vows, but it has everything to do with his situation. Jephthah's vow represents a worst case scenario. The advice is simple. Avoid vows, because vows must be kept.

## Medieval Commentary:
## Midrash

A related body of medieval rabbinic commentary is termed "midrash." Midrash comes from the Hebrew root *drš,* meaning "to search" or "to search for meaning." Midrash refers to both a process of interpretation and a body of literature, most of it dating from 400 to 1200 C.E. In rabbinic

---

[6] Rabinowitz, "Vows and Vowing," 228.

[7] Joseph Telushkin, *The Book of Jewish Values* (New York: Bell Tower, 2000) 458.

commentary there is a distinction between interpretation of law *(halakah)* and interpretation of narrative *(aggadah)*. *Aggadah* includes a variety of literary forms, such as parables, ethical illustrations, legends, allegories, and homilies. The Torah contains both law and narrative; the Mishnah is largely *halakah;* and the Talmud covers both.

Midrash is composed of various forms of *aggadah* and can be used to interpret legal texts as well as narrative texts. For example, the legal text found in the mishnaic tractate *Mo'ed* deals with the shofar, the horn blown on Rosh Hashanah (Jewish New Year). The Mishnah states that the horn must come from certain animals and not others. A prior source for the tradition of blowing the horn comes, in part, from Gen 22:13, where Abraham sees a ram "caught in a thicket by its horns."[8] Thus a narrative Torah text lies behind a legal text and the connection between the two rests on as little as one word, "horn." The two texts are further linked by a midrashic analogy claiming that just as the ram's horn was caught in the thicket, so the Jews were trapped by oppressive political powers until one day "the Lord God will blow the horn . . . [and] defend them" (*Gen. Rab.* 56.9). This example illustrates how catchwords provide links from narrative to law and back to narrative. This intertwining of texts promotes legal practice by encasing it in tradition.

While the medieval rabbis considered the Torah to be a direct revelation of God, they were also aware that a rigid interpretation would not be in the best interest of Judaism. Therefore they adopted a method of dialogue with the Torah (and Tanakh) that called upon commentators from various locations over several centuries to contribute to ongoing interpretation of the text. This technique reflects the way the Mishnah and Talmud were compiled. Commentators read the Torah through the lens of their changing cultural and political circumstances in an effort to resolve internal issues or the external pressures placed upon their communities. The resulting midrash helped clarify their current circumstances while maintaining connections with the past. This process allowed the whole complex of Judaism to evolve by expanding its boundaries to include many generations in many places simultaneously.[9]

Narrative midrash can be arranged in an abbreviated form, much like the previously illustrated legal material on dietary vows, or it can be arranged as extended midrash. We will illustrate both forms. The first type reads like a text from the Mishnah, with various quotations from rabbis or

---

[8] Barry W. Holtz, "Midrash," in idem, ed., *Back to the Sources,* 179.

[9] Howard Schwartz, *Reimagining the Bible: The Storytelling of the Rabbis* (New York: Oxford University Press, 1998) 6.

sages grouped together to reflect on a portion of the Bible. The following example illustrates how the first verse of Genesis is presented in this format. The lettered statements and questions offer various opinions concerning the familiar text "In the beginning, God created the heavens. . . ." The common theme is the mystery of creation.

> A. Said R. Judah bar Simon, "To begin with, when the world was being created, 'He reveals deep and secret things,' for it is written, 'In the beginning God created the heavens' (Gen 1:1). But the matter was not spelled out.
>
> B. "Where then was it spelled out?
>
> C. "Elsewhere: 'Who stretches out the heaven as a curtain' (Isa 40:22).
>
> D. "'. . . and the earth' (Gen 1:1). But this matter, too, was not then spelled out.
>
> E. "Where then was it spelled out?
>
> F. "Elsewhere: 'For he says to the snow, "Fall on the earth"' (Job 37:6).
>
> G. "'And God said, Let there be light' (Gen 1:3).
>
> H. "And this too was not spelled out.
>
> I. "Where then was it spelled out?
>
> J. "Elsewhere: 'Who covers yourself with light as with a garment' (Ps 104:2)." (*Gen. Rab.* 1.6.4)[10]

Rabbi Judah bar Simon collects and arranges other biblical verses that do not specifically answer the question at hand. At first glance it is difficult to see how these statements relate to Gen 1:1. A closer look that notes the repetition of words, the occurrence of statements versus questions, and proof-texts from Isaiah, Job, and Psalms reveals a pattern in the Midrash. The phrase "spelled out" is repeated six times, three times as a statement in the negative, "not spelled out," followed each time by the question, "Where then was it spelled out?" Each question introduces a biblical quotation dealing with the creation of the sky, snow, and light, and implying God as the creator without any further description. The series of questions and the

---

[10] Quoted in Jacob Neusner, ed., *Genesis Rabbah: The Judaic Commentary to the Book of Genesis* (Atlanta: Scholars, 1985) 1:6. Punctuation as shown. Also see Daniel Boyarin, *Intertextuality and the Reading of Midrash* (Bloomington: Indiana University Press, 1994) 17.

biblical quotations reinforce the idea of the "deep and secret" nature of God's creation of the world. No secrets are revealed, but mystery is maintained. Note also that the rabbis assumed that the Prophets and the Writings were themselves commentary on the Torah, so that it was natural to draw on them.

A second form of midrash is a sustained narrative that contains typical elements of a story—setting, plot, and characters, as discussed in Chapter One. This type of midrash can be as short as a sentence or two filling in a single narrative silence in the biblical story, or it can be an extended midrash that retells most of the biblical story, filling in numerous narrative silences. We will encounter both short and extended midrash in the story of Jephthah's daughter in Chapter Four. At this point, to better understand the relationship of Scripture and midrash, we will explore the narrative of Deborah and Yael in two versions in the Bible and the midrash that enhances that story.

Two women heroes in Judges, Deborah and Yael, capture the imagination of midrashic writers. Deborah is a judge, prophet, and military leader during the period of the tribal confederacy. She receives the word of the LORD and demonstrates her military prowess by commanding a battle against the Canaanites. As they are about to go into battle Deborah warns her general, Barak, that a woman will be the one to capture the enemy, Sisera. Indeed, Yael, a foreigner, insures the Israelite victory by slaying Sisera.

Yael is married to a Kenite and is loyal to the Israelites. In the older poetic version of the story she slays Sisera by hammering a tent peg through his skull (Judg 5:24-27). She does so of her own volition. Apparently she is aware of the political circumstances confronting the Israelites and the Canaanites; she makes a commitment to side with the Israelites. In Judg 5:24 the poet calls her "most blessed of women." The prose version of the narrative, written at a later time (Judg 4:17-22), fills in narrative gaps in the poem with details that reinterpret Yael's action.[11] In this version Yael invites Sisera into her tent and covers him, and as he sleeps she drives a tent peg through his head. In Judges 5 the act does not take place in the tent and Sisera could be either standing or sitting when she kills him, suggesting that she must overcome him with brute strength rather than stealth. It would appear that the later prose story reinterprets the poetic version to imply that Yael uses feminine wiles to entrap Sisera and kill him in his sleep. Hence Yael is not as heroic as she appears in Judges 5. She is not

---

[11] The song of Deborah in Judges 5 is dated by some to the late twelfth century B.C.E., making it one of the oldest sources in the Tanakh. William L. Holladay, *The Psalms Through Three Thousand Years* (Minneapolis: Fortress, 1993) 22.

considered most blessed of women and her character appears to be tainted with sexual innuendo.

The portrait of treachery is enhanced in the rabbinic midrash on this text. In an extended narrative midrash, a first-century writer called Pseudo-Philo heightens the sexual overtones suggested in Judges 4. In Ps.-Philo 31:3-9 Yael invites Sisera into her tent, where the bed is strewn with roses.[12] Exhausted from battle, Sisera requests water. Instead, Yael gives him milk laced with wine to induce sleep. Yael implores God to send her a sign that what she is about to do has divine sanction. Assured that the murder is God's will, she slays Sisera, as in the Judges narratives. As Sisera is dying she taunts him about dying ignominiously at the hands of a woman. When Deborah's general, Barak, arrives on the scene, Yael calls him blessed of God. The heroic and blessed Yael of Judges 5 becomes a conniving, seducing, insulting woman who names a man blessed of God. What kind of hero is she now?

The story in Pseudo-Philo adds nothing to our understanding of the historical circumstances or social realities of tribal relations from 1200–1000 B.C.E., nor does it enrich our understanding of the relationship between ancient Israel and God. It does, however, tell us a great deal about the values, beliefs, and social customs of the first-century author. We can surmise that the author was uncomfortable with Yael, perhaps because she was a foreigner, a strong woman, or someone said to be blessed of God. What better way to degrade her than to associate her action with wanton sexuality? This extended midrash moves well beyond the biblical versions in detail and in intent.

Another function of midrash was to explain changes in values and beliefs.[13] For example, the concept of a soul and afterlife came into Judaism during the Hellenistic period after 332 B.C.E., when most of the Tanakh was already composed. Those who accepted the idea of the soul as an entity separate from the body wrote midrash supporting their view and attached it to selected biblical texts. For example, Micah, an idol maker in the hill country of Ephraim, establishes a shrine housing his idols in Judges 17–18. Idolatry was condemned repeatedly in the Tanakh, and this condemnation is embellished in Ps.-Philo 44:1-10. Here there are torturous punishments for offenders, as well as the statement: "when the soul is separated from the body . . . let us not mourn over these things that we suffer; but because whatever we ourselves have devised, these will we receive." The midrash

---

[12] James H. Charlesworth, ed., "Pseudo-Philo," in idem, ed., *The Old Testament Pseudepigrapha* (Garden City, NY: Doubleday, 1985) 2:297–377.

[13] Holtz, "Midrash," 182.

becomes a vehicle for a new view of the soul and judgment in an afterlife. This illustrates how flexible the midrash can be in shaping new beliefs while maintaining the general outline of the biblical narrative.

Similarly, the midrashim on Jephthah's daughter are concerned with values such as justice, family loyalty, compassion, and adherence to Torah traditions. The rabbis struggle with the social structures that surround the making and keeping of vows. On a more theological level, the rabbis attempt to explore God's withdrawal from the tragedy of the daughter's death. Chapter Six will present a more extended discussion of these issues.

At this point we can draw some conclusions about the nature of midrash. For the most part characters, place names, and plot line from the biblical story are maintained in midrash. Where there is a narrative silence in the biblical story, midrash fills in the gaps. Characters can be added, place names are often explained, connections with other narratives are included, and other episodes are added to enhance the writer's purpose. Material that is added to the original story reflects debates pertinent to the time of the writer. Midrash maintains the theological intent of the original story with respect to belief in a monotheistic god and the history of the Jews as God's people. Although midrash may question the actions of individual characters, the overarching structure of society is maintained. Finally, midrash may reveal ethical concerns that were not part of the original narrative. An outstanding feature of midrash is its emphasis on ethical living in new times and life settings.

## Collections of Midrash

The earliest collections of midrash go back to the early third century C.E. The Tanna'im were rabbis who collected homiletic sayings before the Mishnah was completed. The classical period (400–600) saw such works as *Genesis Rabbah,* which contained a sequential commentary on the entire book of Genesis. The midrash of the middle period (640–1000) produced writings authored by a single person, pseudonymous collections, and collections of sayings artificially attributed to sages of earlier times. The late period (1000–1500) saw large anthologies of midrash. Midrashic literature encompasses twelve centuries and originated in communities all over the Jewish Diaspora.[14] The midrash on Jephthah's daughter comes from each of these periods.

---

[14] Raphael Patai, ed., *Gates To The Old City: A Book of Jewish Legends* (Northvale, NJ: Jason Aronson, 1980) 258.

## Intertextual Reading and Creation of Midrash

In our discussion of the portrayal of Yael in Judges 4 and 5 we noted how the author called Pseudo-Philo combines elements of both narratives to create a new narrative in which he links Yael's killing of Sisera to her use of feminine wiles. The author uses two texts (in this instance containing the same characters and plot) to create new meaning as presented in a midrash. He apparently wants to explain how a woman could act heroically, a characteristic usually attributed to men.

Intertextual reading takes place when one reads one text in light of or alongside another text. The reader observes a relationship between the texts through repetition of words and sentences, as well as textual elements that are transformed to convey new meaning.[15] Intertextuality can involve either the production of a text or the reading of a text. In terms of text production it deals with various sources that have been collected over time and assembled into a larger text. Intertextuality also takes place when a reader puts two texts together by recognizing repetitions and transformations in them. Thus a reader-centered intertextual study sees the autonomy of the individual text and the shared elements that permit a dialogue between them. The reader-centered intertextual approach differs from a historical interpretation in that it accepts the text as a finished product rather than a collection of sources.

Ellen van Wolde outlines a procedure for intertextual study.[16] The first step is to recognize similarities between or among texts. The second step is to list the repetition of words or concepts, stylistic features, themes, character types, and actions. By color coding the texts, as described in Chapter One, it is possible to produce a visual picture of the similarities between them. If there are sufficient similarities one can proceed to the third step, which involves analysis that points out intertextual relationships and new meanings that emerge from the dialogue. In identifying similarities the reader creates connections with a wider reality. In this process the reader will likely choose categories for comparison that reflect a particular reality. For example, in the Pseudo-Philo midrash on Yael the images of a bed strewn with roses and a portrayal of Yael as a conniving woman may indicate a social setting in which women asserted power not in keeping with tradition. If so, Pseudo-Philo read Judges 4 and 5 and merged them with images from his own culture to create a text with a new emphasis.

---

[15] Ellen van Wolde, "Intertextuality: Ruth in Dialogue with Tamar," in Athalya Brenner and Carole Fontaine, eds., *A Feminist Companion to the Bible* (Sheffield: Sheffield Academic Press, 1997) 429.

[16] Ibid. 432.

## An Intertextual Reading of Gen 22:1-19 and Judg 11:29-40

In this section we will illustrate how two biblical stories can be read intertextually and how that reading is related to midrash. One can hardly read the account of Jephthah's daughter without reflecting on a similar narrative in which Abraham nearly sacrifices his son Isaac (Gen 22:1-19). These texts can serve as appropriate conversation partners.

Genesis 22 opens with God testing the patriarch Abraham by telling him to take his only son Isaac to a mountain and there sacrifice him as a burnt offering to God. Abraham agrees to the test. He starts out on the journey taking wood, a donkey, two young men, and his son, trusting that God will show him the correct place to perform the act. En route Abraham and Isaac leave the young men with orders to wait for them, and father and son continue on together. Isaac asks his father where the lamb for the burnt offering is. Abraham replies that God will provide it. Abraham then arranges the wood on the altar and lays his son on top of the wood. As Abraham is about to slay his son, an angel of the LORD stops him, convinced that Abraham fears God. Abraham sees a ram in the thicket, takes it, and offers it as the burnt offering. The angel speaks to Abraham a second time and reiterates the covenant promise that Abraham will be the father of many and the nations of the world will find blessing through his offspring. Abraham returns to the two men and they go to Beersheba.

An intertextual comparison of the two stories shows several key words appearing in both texts. Both involve a father and an only child. Both involve events on a mountain. Both concern a burnt offering of a human being to God. Both narratives mention young men/women companions who serve as partial witnesses to the events.

Thematically the two narratives involve loyalty to God as an initial reason for the burnt offering. In Genesis 22 God tests Abraham. In Judges 11 Jephthah initiates a vow promising a burnt offering if he is successful in battle. The stakes of the offering are high for both Abraham and Jephthah. If Isaac is killed, Abraham will not have an appropriate heir to ensure the continuation of the covenant. The entire enterprise of the nation of Israel and its mandate to be a blessing to all nations is at stake. Jephthah also stands to lose his inheritance, since he has no other offspring. By law his land would go to relatives rather than descendants. In the conclusion of the Jephthah narrative in Judg 12:1-7, intertribal warfare breaks out, threatening the security of the nation. Thus the future of the nation is at risk in both narratives.

Stylistically the two texts contain dialogue between father and child. Both are suspenseful, leaving the reader wondering if God will save the day or not. Both raise important questions about the nature of God. What kind of God is this who tests a father by requiring that he kill his only child? What kind of God requires human sacrifice?

In terms of character types, Abraham and Jephthah are both recognized leaders in Israel. They are expected to uphold high standards of behavior. The son and the daughter in the narratives are obedient to their fathers. Isaac makes a gentle inquiry about the lamb for the burnt offering but raises no other questions. Jephthah's daughter is ready to fulfill her father's vow, asking only for a delay.

The outstanding characteristic common to the two narratives is the willingness of each father to slay his child. Both narratives may leave the reader uncomfortable with respect to parental power and God's power.

In response to God's request, Abraham answers God with the formulaic phrase: "Here I am." He does not ask God for any explanation. He simply makes preparations and sets forth on the journey. Jephthah receives the Spirit of the LORD and then makes an additional bargain with God to ensure victory. Abraham's faithful obedience contrasts with what might be interpreted as Jephthah's lack of faith that requires a bargain. At some point Isaac and Jephthah's daughter become aware that their lives are in jeopardy. Isaac appears slow to understand the gravity of the situation in his inquiry about the lamb. Abraham answers the question with the vague words that the LORD will provide. Jephthah's daughter is fully aware that she will die. Her father tears his clothes, blames her, and confesses the nature of his vow.

At this point there is a significant difference between the texts. Isaac remains silent as he is placed on the pyre, but Jephthah's daughter requests a delay. Isaac is silent; she is vocal on her own behalf. We might imagine Isaac speaking up on his own behalf and bargaining with his father. With the covenant at stake, might he not ask that his execution be delayed? Let him marry and have sons first. At any rate, Isaac's silent acquiescence and Abraham's persistence bring about God's intervention to save Isaac. There is no divine intervention to save Jephthah's daughter. In fact, God, who was behind the scenes throughout the Abraham narrative, is merely named in association with the victory over the Ammonites and is passively associated with Jephthah's vow. Otherwise God is absent in the account in Judges.

Although events occur on a mountain in both texts, the descriptions are quite different. Great detail surrounds the preparation for the sacrifice of Isaac and this serves to delay the ultimate act. As elsewhere in the Bible, the mountain in the Genesis scene becomes a place of communication with God. Just as Moses receives the Ten Commandments on Mount Sinai, Abraham encounters an angel of God and is told that the covenant will proceed. Jephthah's daughter spends two months in the mountains with her friends, but no information is given about their activities. If mountaintops are places of communication with the deity, it is left to our imagination to speculate about what happens among the women. Perhaps the women gained insight into the nature of the deity. Possibilities abound. Did they see a God who favored men over women? Did they experience God removed from everyday life? Did they come to experience the spirit of God in their support of each other? Did they come to appreciate the complexity of human relationships? Did they have to reshape their idea of the relationship between God and humanity?

A central goal of intertextual analysis is to find new meanings that arise from the conversation between the texts. Here the dialogue raises questions about the relationship between fathers and God and the consequences for their offspring. Do fathers perceive God correctly when the consequences are a matter of life and death? Why does God interact only with individuals in these texts? It appears that in both narratives the voice of the larger social community is lacking. For that matter, the voice of the mother is missing as well. No one challenges or advises Abraham or Jephthah. What does this intertextual reading suggest about victims and near-victims? Isaac will go on to be the bearer of the covenant without so much as a hint that he experienced this trauma. Jephthah's daughter lives with her impending death for two months. What effect will this trauma have on her friends who are with her during that time? Will daughters be more fearful of their fathers? Will the narrative become a rallying point for women to work out their fears together?

The conversation between these two texts enables readers to identify narrative gaps. We can attempt to fill narrative silences in one text with material or themes from the other and, in so doing, recognize opportunities for midrash. For centuries the rabbis have supplied narratives to fill these gaps. In Chapter Seven we will note how modern readers can do this as well.

## A Midrashic Reading of Gen 22:1-19

At this point another voice enters the dialogue. In the conversation above we noted that the author of Gen 22:1-19 described in detail the preparation for the journey, the journey itself, Isaac's query about the need for a sacrificial lamb, and the actual binding of Isaac on the pyre. With all the detailed description leading up to the scene in which Abraham holds the knife above his son, it seems odd that there is almost no reported conversation between father and son. We might wonder why Isaac says so little. Surely he must know that he is to be the sacrifice. Perhaps he, like

Jephthah's daughter, is just going along with the plan. If we accept Isaac's silence we see a compliant child doing what needs to be done. However, if we view this as a real-life scenario with a real father (instead of a "biblical" father) and a real son instead of the heir to the covenant, we wonder what conversation might have taken place. Was Isaac willing to become a sacrifice? Did he panic? Did he try to escape? The ancient rabbis wondered about this as well. Through midrash they responded by creating a new story that fills in narrative silences in an older story.

So, what conversation might have taken place between Isaac and Abraham? According to *Tanhuma* 23, Isaac trembled violently when he saw that there was nothing for the sacrifice.

> He asked again, "Where is the lamb for the burnt-offering?" Abraham responded: "Since you ask, the Holy One, blessed be He, has selected you." "If he has chosen me," Isaac replied, "I shall willingly surrender my soul to Him, but I am gravely concerned about my mother." Nevertheless, they went both of them together (Gen 22:8), of one mind: convinced that one was to slaughter and the other to be slaughtered. . . . As Abraham was about to slaughter him, Isaac cried out, "Father, bind my hands and feet, for the will to live is strong within me, and when I see the knife descending, I may tremble and the offering may become defective (as a result of the knife slipping). Abraham stretched forth his hand and took the knife to slay his son. . . . Isaac said to him, "Father, do not tell my mother about this while she is standing at the edge of a pit or a roof lest she hurl herself down and die."[17]

As Abraham is about to slay Isaac, a messenger intervenes, causing the knife to fall. Abraham reaches out to take the knife. A voice from heaven says, "Lay not your hand upon the lad" (Gen 22:12). If this had not happened, Isaac would certainly have been sacrificed.[18]

In another midrash Isaac is portrayed as a willing sacrifice. Isaac says:

> Yet have I not been born into the world to be offered as a sacrifice to him who made me? Now my blessedness will be above that of all men, because there will be nothing like this; and about me future generations will be instructed and through me the peoples will understand

---

[17] Samuel A. Berman, ed., *Midrash Tanhuma Yelammedenu* (Hoboken: Ktav Publishing, 1996) 146. See *Genesis Rabbah* 55–56 for another midrash on this narrative.

[18] The midrash continues with Sarah finding out about Abraham's act, being overcome with the news, and dying on the spot.

that the LORD has made the soul of a man worthy to be a sacrifice (Ps.-Philo 32:3).

In both midrashim Isaac is willing to die. In the Pseudo-Philo text his death will be efficacious for future generations.

## A Midrashic Reading of Judg 11:29-40

Now let us add yet another voice to the conversation. An extended midrash on Judges 11 is found in Pseudo-Philo 40. Speaking to her father, the daughter recalls the incident when Isaac was to be offered as a sacrifice. She says that Isaac did not refuse Abraham, but "gladly gave consent to him and that the one being offered was ready and the one who was offering was rejoicing." Since this conversation is not contained in the biblical story, it is evident that the midrash writers freely borrowed from other stories to enhance their own midrash.

This multilayered conversation shows how an ancient text has been cast into new configurations to enhance an understanding of values and to probe the nature of God. The strategy of reading a biblical narrative against another narrative or writing a midrash on the narrative opens up multiple possibilities for finding meaning in the Bible.

## Summary

In this chapter we have explored ancient forms of commentary on the Bible. Since the first century the rabbis have interpreted Torah laws and narratives freely, borrowing texts from other parts of the Tanakh and from folklore to create new tradition. Thus the meaning of the Tanakh was continually updated. Two examples are of particular interest in the following chapters of this book. Torah laws regarding vows are redefined in the Mishnah and in subsequent midrash on Judges 11 (see Chapter Four). We are also concerned with the position of women in these ancient texts as illustrated by the biblical versions of the story of Yael and the midrash on those narratives. Yael is blessed of women in Judges 5, only to be portrayed as a conniving female in Pseudo-Philo. How does tradition treat Jephthah's daughter? Is she defined solely on the basis of her subordinate position in patriarchal Israel? In the next chapter we will add modern feminist voices to our conversation. What is a feminist critique of the Bible and how does Jephthah's daughter figure in this critique?

# CHAPTER THREE

*Feminist Critique as a Conversation Partner*

The description of the role of women in ancient Israel in Chapter One paves the way for a feminist interpretation of the Bible. Feminist interpretation recognizes a disparity in the distribution of power between men and women in the biblical text itself, in subsequent interpretations, and in modern-day social and religious institutions. In this chapter we will begin with a brief history of feminist interpretation. We will then discuss characteristics of feminist interpretation and different expressions of feminist critique, illustrating them with biblical narratives.

Nineteenth century women's rights advocates, such as Elizabeth Cady Stanton (1815–1902), recognized that the Bible has been used throughout history to deny women equal status with men.[1] Stanton published *The Woman's Bible* in 1895, in which she blamed the Bible and religious institutions for the economic, social, and sexual oppression of women.[2] Stanton was severely criticized for her position even by her closest friends and coworkers. After the publication of *The Women's Bible* there was no further concerted critical analysis of the Bible with regard to women's equality until the latter half of the twentieth century.

On the heels of the sexual revolution of the 1960s many women began to seek equality with men in such areas as education, economics, politics, and religious institutions. Feminists, who as a group include both men and

---

[1] For a history of feminist biblical criticism prior to Stanton see Gerda Lerner, *The Creation of Feminist Consciousness: From the Middle Ages to Eighteen-Seventy* (New York: Oxford University Press, 1993) 138–66.

[2] Elizabeth Cady Stanton, *The Woman's Bible* (Boston: Northeastern University Press, 1993) viii.

women, advocate that women receive the same rights granted to men in society. Feminism also recognizes that most if not all social systems are patriarchal, i.e., they assume a form of social organization in which males hold dominant power and determine what part females will or will not play. Feminism critiques these social systems and works to restructure them equitably for both women and men.[3]

A feminist critique of religious institutions reveals that, like secular institutions, they are historically patriarchal and hierarchical in structure. Feminist women and men seek equality by demanding increased participation of women among the clergy, a dismantling of hierarchical structures, and a reconstruction of theology that has reinforced male domination and male images of God. Because much of theology is based on the Bible or its interpretation, examination of biblical texts from a feminist perspective has grown since the mid-1970s.

Feminist critique of the Bible acknowledges that it was written by men in ancient patriarchal societies and consequently promotes a patriarchal ordering of religious/civil institutions. For example, in Judg 11:1–12:7 Jephthah, a judge in Israel, has military and political authority within what some scholars call the tribal confederacy. He is remembered for his military success in defeating the Ammonites, which ensures the security of the tribal confederacy, at least for a while. Centuries later, in a New Testament text, Jephthah is honored as one who through faith conquered kingdoms, administered justice, and was mighty in war (Heb 11:32-33). In Hebrews he is only remembered as a warrior, with no mention of his sacrifice of his daughter. When feminist interpreters read the Judges 11 story they shift the focus of their study from the hero Jephthah to his daughter. For them the daughter, who was either forgotten or kept at the periphery of the story, occupies center stage. She is not merely a willing victim of her father's vow; she is a pivotal character through whom readers can critique systems of male domination.

## Characteristics of Feminist Biblical Interpretation

The women portrayed in biblical narratives are not so much historical as representational in that their stories reflect social norms in ancient Israel. The narratives portray characters that exhibit accepted and unaccepted be-

---

[3] In some circles feminism is equated with "man hating" or "male bashing." That is not the intent of this term, either historically or in this work. Some would prefer that a more gender-neutral term be found that would be less controversial. However, the term "feminism" calls attention to the inequalities that cannot be neutralized by changing the language. Feminism calls for active involvement in bringing about just systems for women.

havior.[4] Cultural roles assigned to women and men become established in subsequent generations partly because of the influence of the Bible as sacred text. A feminist analysis attempts to use these same narratives to expose power inequities that have survived even in modern times.

## Female Characters Created by Male Authors

Feminist critique recognizes that female characters in biblical narratives are largely creations of male authors and reflect men's understanding of women. For example, in 2 Sam 11:2-5 the author describes Bathsheba as a beautiful woman who happens to be taking a bath when King David spies her. Messengers arrive to take her to the king, who impregnates her and arranges for her husband to die in battle. Traditional interpreters, including numerous artists, have often assumed that Bathsheba was soliciting the king's attention and willing to commit adultery. There is no indication of this in the narrative. An alternative view, held by some feminist interpreters, picks up on the voyeuristic theme in the text, noting that Bathsheba's body is the focus of the story.[5] Interpreters who portray Bathsheba seducing David may be attempting to excuse his appalling behavior by casting blame on the woman.

## Searching for a Woman's Voice

Feminist interpretation acknowledges that it is not possible to reconstruct a biblical narrative from a woman's perspective. However, it is possible to expose the dominant male voice of the narrative, thus allowing us to discern a missing female voice. We cannot know Bathsheba's version of the encounter with David, but we can retell the story from her point of view, using only the details in the narrative. Her version might be as follows: One afternoon I was bathing when a messenger from the king summoned me and brought me to the king. We had sex together, then I returned to my house. I became pregnant and notified the king. My husband was killed in battle and I became the king's wife.

This retelling exposes the power differential between Bathsheba and David. David had the power and authority to bring her to his home, have sex with her, and cover up the deed by having her husband killed. Most likely Bathsheba had no other choice than to comply with the king's

---

[4] J. Cheryl Exum, *Fragmented Women: Feminist (Sub)versions of Biblical Narratives* (Valley Forge, PA: Trinity Press International, 1993) 171.
[5] Ibid. 175.

wishes. No dialogue is given to Bathsheba in this narrative, but her plight can be discerned.

As much as many of us would like to rewrite a biblical narrative from a woman's perspective, it is not possible. Not only are ancient resources for such a rewriting unavailable, but within Jewish and Christian traditions the text of the Bible is considered closed. The Bible is canon (a selection of unalterable texts) that is authoritative for both Jews (Tanakh) and Christians (Old Testament and New Testament). Rather than rewrite the text, we are free to explore various means of interpretation.

## Recognizing Narrative Silences

The recognition of narrative silences in a text is often a point of entry into the world of women. The lack of information about Bathsheba's circumstance leads us to wonder whether she could have refused to go to David. Was there anyone else residing with her to offer protection? Was she raped? Could she appeal to a court? What laws were in place to protect women in these circumstances? Such questions highlight the male-centered nature of biblical narrative and the androcentric world in which it was written.

Traditionally, male readers have noted narrative silences in biblical stories and have filled in the gaps with midrash or reflection that reveals their own attitudes toward women in general. Some of the medieval rabbis sought justice for wronged women in the midrash they produced, while others ignored women's plight altogether. In the case of David and Bathsheba the midrash focuses on David's guilt, claiming that he wept every hour and "ate his bread with ashes." There is excessive attention given to David's frame of mind, while Bathsheba is only the occasion of his sin.[6] In other places the rabbis are sympathetic to the plight of women. We will see that in some of the midrash on Jephthah's daughter the rabbis are attentive to her need for justice.

## Feminist Interpretation Rooted in Women's Experience

The questions raised by feminist readers arise out of women's personal experience of oppression or inequality. Women who have been raped are likely to be quick to see the power inequity illustrated in the stories of Bathsheba and David, Tamar and Amnon (2 Samuel 13), and the Levite's

---

[6] Louis Ginzberg, *Legends of the Bible* (Philadelphia: Jewish Publication Society, 1956) 547.

wife (Judges 19). Women who have been abused may readily connect with Jephthah's daughter. Personal experience is valued in feminist scholarship in that it enlivens the questions brought to the text. Caution, however, is in order. Feminist critique must be accompanied by the same scholarship and methodology as other forms of biblical interpretation.

Initially, feminist critique arose among white, middle-class, educated, and socially advantaged women. Over time women from other races, ethnic backgrounds, and social classes claimed that feminism ignored the particular experiences of oppression within these other groups, which included African-American, Asian, and Hispanic/Latina women. Feminists now recognize that interpretations will vary according to the ethnicity, social status, religious affiliation, and age of the interpreter. An African-American woman might imagine Bathsheba as a slave woman, who would have even less legal recourse than a free person. Today feminists realize that biblical interpretations from multiple social and ethnic locations contribute to a broader understanding of the Bible and the varied forms of sexism in all cultures.

In a feminist interpretation of the narrative of Jephthah's daughter it is assumed that the text was written by a male author who made various choices, e.g., by leaving her unnamed, determining her range of activities, giving her speech, and omitting crucial elements of the story. The author created a story that supported patriarchal interests. Jephthah's position as a judge is not threatened, even though he engages in human sacrifice. His daughter is portrayed as a good girl who, for the most part, complies with the house rules by not overtly challenging the patriarchal system.

## Critics of Feminist Interpretation

Criticism of feminist interpretation of the Bible involves a number of points. Elisabeth Schüssler Fiorenza describes these as roadblocks to understanding feminist interpretation.[7] For some the word "feminism" itself seems divisive in that it appears to favor women over men, merely reversing the inequality inherent in patriarchy. Some assume that feminism is only for women when, in fact, many men identify themselves as feminists as well. Some see feminism as monolithic, not realizing that it has become more diverse, incorporating a spectrum of viewpoints. Some critics agree with Elizabeth Cady Stanton that the Bible and religion are

---

[7] Elisabeth Schüssler Fiorenza, *Wisdom Ways: Introducing Feminist Biblical Interpretation* (Maryknoll, NY: Orbis, 2001) 53–74. See the footnotes in this section of *Wisdom Ways* for specific criticisms of feminist interpretation.

anti-woman, yet many women are trying to work constructively within the structures of institutional religion to bring about change. Others contend that feminist interpretation of the Bible is too academic and not accessible to lay people. Still other critics focus on their belief about the nature of the Bible itself—that it is the direct word of God and not open to different forms of interpretation.

My position is to support the goal of feminism to bring about a more just and equitable world for both women and men. I do not support the position of those who claim the Bible and religion are, in essence, anti-woman and that the Bible is too patriarchal to be of value for women. Examples of this view are advanced by scholars such as Naomi Goldenberg, who claims that the Bible is an antiquated text that must be left behind in the interest of creating new symbols, realities, and myths that speak to women.[8] This rejectionist position finds hope in other directions, such as goddess religions, pagan practices, and witch (Wicca) religions, but I contend that the Bible still has value for women today. Just as many writers composed texts that found their way into the Bible, so there are many ways of interpreting the Bible. No one method exhausts the multilayered meanings expressed in the Bible. A feminist interpretation, in concert with liberationist and post-colonial interpretations, is concerned with examining systems of power and domination.

## Multicultural Feminism

Feminism recognizes the cross-cultural need to overcome the oppression of women. This implies that women who identify themselves differently (African-American, Asian, Christian, Hispanic/Latina, Jewish, or lesbian) share a common desire for liberation. Multicultural feminism calls for respectful dialogue among different ethnic groups, races, religions, and sexual orientations. Respectful listening requires that each group maintain an open mind to the unique struggles within other groups. For example, African-American women, like white women, recognize their social location within a white, male-dominated world, but they encounter a world dominated in addition by African-American males and white females. While African-American women and white women share the broad goal of social transformation, African-American women view their social position through the lens of slavery and its aftermath. African-American women have suffered abuse from white mistresses and their counterparts since Reconstruction. The reality of inequality between white women and women

---

[8] Naomi Goldenberg, *Changing of the Gods* (Boston: Beacon, 1979) 10.

of color remains today. When white women are confronted with this reality they are likely to deny the element of racism that is embedded in our culture.

Multicultural feminism also recognizes that within each socially identified group there are subgroups that may or may not be concerned with a feminist agenda. For example, some white women who are not required to work outside the home may be content to adapt to a male-dominated life. Working women who have chosen to follow their own careers might feel that the woman who remains at home is undermining the feminist cause. Feminism today is dealing with these issues.

Of the multicultural feminisms listed above, I will discuss three—namely womanist and mujerista/Latina feminisms, which grow out of liberation theology, and Jewish feminism, which grows out of the particular experience of Jewish women.

Liberation theology assumes that God desires freedom for all human beings. It finds expression in liberationist movements, both social and political in nature, in which the oppressed come to realize their own oppression and work to create a new social reality. Since religious institutions are largely modeled after hierarchical social institutions, they, too, are in need of transformation. A liberationist interpretation of the Bible emphasizes certain biblical passages that speak of finding freedom from oppression, such as the liberation of the Hebrew slaves from Egypt in Exodus and teachings of Jesus in the gospels that highlight the radical nature of the reign of God.[9]

## Womanist Interpretation

According to Delores Williams, a womanist interpretation is concerned with the faith, survival, and freedom struggle of African-American women.[10] Alice Walker, author of *The Color Purple,* coined the term "womanist." It refers to "a black feminist or feminist of color."[11] Walker includes all women of color in her definition, saying "womanist is to feminist as purple is to lavender." Womanist critique is deeply concerned with

[9] See Stephen J. Patterson's discussion of Jesus' message of the empire (reign) of God as an egalitarian reality on earth as opposed to the hierarchical empire of Rome in *The God of Jesus: The Historical Jesus & the Search for Meaning* (Harrisburg, PA: Trinity Press International, 1998) 86.

[10] Delores S. Williams, *Sisters in the Wilderness: The Challenge of Womanist God-Talk* (Maryknoll, NY: Orbis, 1993) xiv.

[11] Alice Walker, *In Search of Our Mothers' Gardens* (New York: Harcourt, Brace, Jovanovich, 1983) xi–xii.

the realities of social class, economic inequities, and political issues that are embedded in the everyday lives of women of color.

As noted above, feminist analysis grows out of women's experience of oppression or inequality. As an African-American, Delores Williams recognizes that the story of Abraham depicts the plight of Sarah, his wife. Sarah is old and barren and thus seemingly unable to provide a son to carry on the lineage that will fulfill the covenant between God and Abraham. However, another woman, Hagar, an Egyptian slave, is integral to Sarah's plan (Gen 16:1-16; 21:1-21). The covenant stated that God would make a great nation out of Abraham's offspring. Sarah, recognizing her own limitations, gives Hagar to Abraham as a wife so that she can bear him a son. Once Hagar is pregnant, rivalry between the women results in Hagar fleeing to the wilderness. There she encounters an angel of the LORD, who tells her to return to her mistress. The angel names the child in Hagar's womb "Ishmael" and foreshadows his fate as an outsider and a warrior. Hagar names God "El-Roi" (God of Seeing) and then returns to Sarah. In her old age Sarah gives birth to Isaac, who will become the true bearer of the covenant. She is jealous when she sees Ishmael and Isaac playing together and insists that Abraham banish Hagar and Ishmael. With God's consent, Abraham sends them into the wilderness with only bread and a skin of water. As Ishmael is dying, Hagar encounters God, who enables her to see a well of water to save her son. Ishmael grows up, marries an Egyptian woman, and becomes an expert with the bow.

Williams sees in Hagar a woman whose story intersects with the experience of African-American women during the period slavery in the United States and its aftermath.[12] Williams reads the narrative from the point of view of the abused Hagar, with the goal of highlighting not only oppression but also strategies for survival. She reads narrative silences with the goal of producing practical strategies for liberation.

According to Williams, the aim of the redactors of the Genesis narratives was to maintain God's intent that the covenant with Abraham and the Hebrews would survive.[13] However, she focuses on another factor that is apparent in Genesis 16 and 21, namely classism (a free woman versus a slave woman). Sarah oppresses Hagar to the point that Hagar seeks freedom in the wilderness and, in her flight, risks punishment for running away. As a runaway surrogate mother, Hagar defies her mistress' plan, as well as Abraham's need for a son and God's intent that the lineage continue through Abraham's offspring. As good as freedom may sound, Hagar is a

[12] Williams, *Sisters in the Wilderness,* 2.
[13] Ibid. 18.

pregnant woman alone in the wilderness. The angel of the LORD escalates her oppression by sending her back to Abraham and Sarah. What kind of God is this who sends the liberated back into oppression? At this point it would seem that Hagar has to choose between inevitable death in the wilderness or a life of abuse with her oppressors.[14]

Although Sarah does bear Isaac, she fears that Ishmael, the firstborn son, will inherit. By implication, Sarah's own status would be diminished.[15] This time the impoverished slave and her son are banished to the wilderness. Williams notes that the biblical narrative gives credit to God for their survival, but it is the faith, hope, and struggle of a homeless woman that enable Hagar, the African slave, to survive. Other issues, including surrogacy, motherhood, rape, homelessness, and economic and sexual oppression are a part of the Hagar narrative.[16]

It is possible to read Genesis 16 and 21 from a feminist perspective that stresses Sarah's ingenuity in attempting to solve her problem of barrenness in her desire to fulfill the covenant, but such an analysis fails to recognize the distinctions of class oppression, ethnic difference, and social privilege. These latter issues are of major concern in womanist interpretation but are often neglected by feminist interpreters who are white, middle-class, educationally privileged, and free from a heritage of slavery. While both feminists and womanists seek equality in a patriarchal world, it is womanist critique that broadens the scope of the task.

My method for analyzing the narrative of Jephthah's daughter is similar to Williams' analysis in that we both approach the story recognizing the subordination of the woman in the text to dominant systems of power. We both note narrative silences in the text, linking them to the experience of today's women. While Williams uses her critique to promote a social action agenda, my goal is to use narrative silences as a window for creating midrash, or "a story within the story," which highlights social values.

## Mujerista Interpretation

Mujerista/Latina theology originated in the social and political liberation movements in the Americas in the second half of the twentieth century. (The term "mujerista" comes from the Spanish word *mujer,* meaning

---

[14] Ibid. 22.

[15] Williams cites legal texts from surrounding Near Eastern cultures to support this thesis namely that should Sarah become a widow her status and economic security could be in jeopardy. Ibid. 27.

[16] Ibid. 33.

woman.) This theology developed as a grassroots movement within the private sphere of women's everyday lives. According to Ada Maria Isasi-Diaz, experiencing women's struggle for survival is the primary task of the mujerista/Latina movement; finding roots for that struggle in the Bible is secondary.[17] The mujerista movement developed from Hispanic Catholicism and was influenced by African and native cultures in which the Bible played only a minor role. Isasi-Diaz claims that mujeristas value their experience of prayer, whether it is to God, Mary, or the saints, as a more direct means of religious inspiration than the Bible, which must be interpreted. In recent years Protestant churches have brought the Bible to Latin America and the mujerista movement. Stories from the Bible are invoked insofar as they speak of oppressive circumstances of Latina/Hispanic women. Biblical stories provide what Isasi-Diaz calls an "interpretive key" that helps one to ask questions rather than to provide one with answers to issues of injustice.

For example, the narrative of Shiphrah and Puah in Exod 1:15-22 serves as an interpretive key to how oppressed women can work for liberation in situations that seem to have rendered them powerless. The narrative takes place in Egypt when the Hebrews are enslaved by the Egyptians. Fearing that the Hebrews will become too numerous and rebel against their oppressors, Pharaoh orders the midwives to kill all the Hebrew male children at birth. The midwives report to Pharaoh that the Hebrew women are vigorous and give birth before the midwife arrives. The narrator informs us that in actuality they are disobeying Pharaoh and protecting the Hebrew infants. The midwives are given credit for their faith in God that results in the birth of even more Hebrew children. "And because the midwives feared God, he gave them families" (Exod 1:19, 21). Pharaoh then orders that all male newborns be thrown into the Nile. When Moses' mother can no longer hide him, three women play strategic roles in assuring the survival of the Hebrew liberator: Pharaoh's daughter rescues the infant Moses from the Nile, and Moses' sister finds a wet nurse in the person of Moses' mother.

A mujerista reading of this narrative stresses the consequences of the brave and risky behavior of the midwives. Their "fear" in Exod 1:19 is an expression of trust in divine holiness. As a result the midwives become life-givers, and the command to kill Hebrew babies is reversed. Isasi-Diaz

[17] Ada Maria Isasi-Diaz, *Mujerista Theology* (Maryknoll, NY: Orbis, 1996) 149. Maria Pilar Aquino prefers the term feminist to mujerista because there are no mujerista political movements in the United States or in Latin America. See "Latina Feminist Theology: Central Features," in eadem, ed., *A Reader in Latina Feminist Theology: Religion and Justice* (Austin: University of Texas Press, 2002) 136.

draws a broader conclusion, saying that the actions of the midwives made the Exodus possible. There can be no liberation without the courage to act and a willingness to risk. These women were indeed risk-takers, agents of their own history and the history of their people.[18]

Mujerista interpretation, like other liberationist interpretations, begins with women's lived experience that finds expression in a biblical story; the story helps women articulate questions that contribute to overt strategies for implementing liberation. This process enables mujeristas/Latinas to assess situations and seek opportunities for self-determination for themselves and their communities. The mujerista critique asks practical questions, such as what sacrifices need to be made. At a theological level mujeristas ask questions such as how God can be the God both of the oppressed and of the oppressor. The tension then is between their allegiance to liberation and what Isasi-Diaz labels their "Hispanic-ness." Can liberation be achieved while maintaining cultural identity? These and many other questions weave what Isasi-Diaz calls a "tapestry of the whole."

Although womanist and mujerista/Latina theologies have similar goals, they differ in their approach to the Bible. Womanist theology is more interested in finding liberation themes in the Bible, undoubtedly from the close association African-Americans have had with the Bible during and since their experience of slavery. Mujeristas/Latinas have seen the Bible as secondary to the task of liberation. However, as Protestant and evangelical traditions become more prominent in Latin America, biblical interpretation will likely become a more central component of the movement.

## Jewish Feminist Interpretation

Under the umbrella of multicultural feminism, Jewish feminism seeks both to identify itself with the agenda of other feminisms, including Christian, womanist, and mujerista, and yet to be distinct from them. In reflecting on her book, *Standing Again at Sinai: Judaism from a Feminist Perspective,* published in 1990, Judith Plaskow acknowledges that her association with Christian feminists has to some degree submerged her Jewish voice. She also claims to harmonize the range of differences among Jewish feminists in this book.[19] The task is to identify what is particular to Jewish feminism and a Jewish feminist interpretation of the Bible. One important

---

[18] Ibid. 164.
[19] Judith Plaskow, "Dealing with Difference Without and Within," *Journal of Feminist Studies in Religion* (Spring 2003) 91–95.

difference is the issue of anti-Judaism/anti-Semitism, spoken or unspoken, that fails to acknowledge that Judaism, from the biblical period through the medieval rabbis to the present day, must be respected as a religion in and of itself, apart from Christianity. A second issue concerns the relationship between the biblical text and midrash. Many Jews have grown up with the midrashic stories as part of their culture and need to learn to differentiate what is in the Bible and what is not.

The emergence of Jewish feminism parallels two twentieth-century milestones in Jewish women's struggle for equality. The first was allowing a girl to become a *bat mitzvah* (literally, "daughter of the commandments"), and the second was ordaining women as rabbis. Since the fourteenth century boys had marked their coming of age with a ceremony called the *bar mitzvah*. The first ceremony recognizing a girl as a *bat mitzvah* occurred in 1922. The bar/bat mitzvah ceremony signifies that the young person has become a responsible Jew. The second milestone occurred when Sally Priesand was ordained a rabbi in 1972. She completed studies at a seminary, like male rabbis, and was then equipped to function as a rabbi. *Bat mitzvah* and ordination opened new opportunities for study and leadership formerly closed to Jewish women. It should be noted that women in Reform, Reconstructionist, and Conservative Judaism have experienced these changes. Orthodox Judaism still does not allow *bat mitzvah*s for girls or ordination for women.

For many Jewish women ordination is a symbol of equality that recognizes the intellectual life of women and their contributions to the community. In the past twenty-five years Jewish women have explored the Tanakh and rabbinic texts as scholars and as activists within their communities. At this stage in its development Jewish feminist interpretation can be classified into three categories—rejectionist, inventive, and revisionist. According to Elyse Goldstein, a rejectionist position claims that the Torah cannot be salvaged; since it is so deeply patriarchal, it cannot speak of women's experience.[20] An inventive position maintains that where women's voices are absent one can create or invent interpretation or midrash to fill the gaps. The revisionist's position invites the reader to reread the Bible with non-patriarchal eyes, using the tools of traditional critical analysis to expose and topple sexism in the text and in the tradition. This position maintains that women in the Torah are portrayed in much the same way as men, with the same strengths and weaknesses. (The differences between biblical men and women, then, are due to the social ordering

---

[20] Elyse Goldstein, *ReVisions: Seeing Torah Through a Feminist Lens* (Woodstock, VT: Jewish Lights, 1998) 28. See the reference to Naomi Goldenberg above.

of the sexes over centuries.) Goldstein maintains that biblical exegesis and the creative act of modern midrash are what keep the tradition vital.

According to Rachel Adler, feminist critique can heal old divisions while finding new ways of reclaiming the holiness of the Torah.[21] The first step in dismantling oppression is to articulate the experience by raising pertinent ethical and moral questions that are at the heart of the biblical text and Judaism in general. For example, following Abraham's near sacrifice of Isaac in Genesis 22, Sarah's death is briefly recorded. Attention is then focused on Abraham's negotiations to purchase a burial plot. A feminist reader might wonder about the significance of Sarah's life and why nothing is said about the circumstances of her death. A medieval midrash suggests that Sarah died immediately after hearing that Abraham nearly sacrificed Isaac. Rona Shapiro notes that in traditional commentary Abraham is praised for his allegiance to God, which goes beyond the ties of kinship.[22] He is willing to sacrifice his child at the request of God. On the other hand, in the midrash Sarah questions the nature of a God who demands the sacrifice of a child. Shapiro claims that Sarah knows that the ethical principles guiding human relations are the essence of God's commandments; they are greater than a single transcendent experience of God on a mountaintop. After Sarah's death Abraham finds a wife for Isaac, remarries, and has no more transcendent experiences of God. Is it Sarah's death that forces Abraham into a more real, human vision of life?

Shapiro uses both inventive and revisionist methods in her interpretation of this text. She draws upon ancient midrash to support her questions probing the very nature of God. Her conclusion calls for a reexamination of ethical systems within Judaism, systems that can no longer be cloaked in pious rhetoric. The goal of the revisionist Jewish critique moves beyond Judaism itself to the healing of the world, known in Hebrew as *tikkun olam.*

## Five Feminist Voices, Five Views of Genesis 1–3

In this section we will engage five feminist interpreters in a discussion of Genesis 1–3. Each interpreter comes to the text from a different experience, uses a different methodology, and has a different goal in mind. All of them acknowledge the patriarchal nature of the text and its influence for women today.

---

[21] Rachel Adler, *Engendering Judaism: An Inclusive Theology and Ethics* (Boston: Beacon, 1998) xxv.

[22] Rona Shapiro, "Woman's Life, Woman's Truth," in Elyse Goldstein, ed., *The Woman's Torah Commentary* (Woodstock, VT: Jewish Lights, 2000) 71.

Probably the most controversial biblical text that relates to women's lives past and present is Genesis 1–3. These chapters contain two creation narratives. The first, known among critical scholars as the Priestly creation narrative, is found in Gen 1:1–2:4a. It speaks of God creating the world in six days and resting on the seventh. After creating the earth, animal life, and plant life, God creates human beings on the sixth day. The second creation narrative, labeled by critics as the Yahwist narrative, occurs in Gen 2:4b–3:24. It describes the creation of a being formed from the earth and the creation of a second being from the rib of the first. The bifurcated sexes, man and woman, are the result of the surgery God performs. The man and the woman disobey God's commandment not to eat the fruit of the tree of knowledge of good and evil. After they eat the fruit they suffer serious consequences, including a life of hard labor for the man, pain in childbearing for the woman, and expulsion from the Garden of Eden. The Yahwist narrative has been used to justify the secondary status of women and misogynistic behavior.

Judith Plaskow, whose essay, "The Coming of Lilith," prompted feminist biblical interpretation in the 1970s, describes an early attempt to create a theology of women that would sustain a movement for equality within institutional religion.[23] Recognizing that a meaningful theology had to grow out of personal experience, women met to tell stories of their own oppression. Through storytelling they recognized common elements and came to value their own experience and the experiences of others. This consciousness-raising is similar to what is described in womanist and mujerista theology. The women realized that it was within a community of women or sisterhood that they could find strength to work for institutional change. Searching for a ritual or myth that would speak of their experience of solidarity, they fashioned a new version of an old midrash telling the tale of Adam's first wife, Lilith.

In the older medieval version of the midrash, God, not wanting Adam to be alone, creates a woman for him from the earth and calls her Lilith. Adam and Lilith argue about who will lie beneath and who will lie above during sexual intercourse. Lilith assumes that the two of them are equal since they were both formed from the earth. Lilith becomes angry and blasphemes by uttering the holy name of God. She then leaves the garden. Adam asks God for help, and God sends three angels to bring her back. Refusing to return, she assumes a demonic role and claims that she was

[23] Judith Plaskow, "The Coming of Lilith: Toward a Feminist Theology," in Carol P. Christ and Judith Plaskow, eds., *Womanspirit Rising: A Feminist Reader in Religion* (San Francisco: Harper & Row, 1979) 198.

created to weaken newborn children. She bargains with the angels, and they agree that when a child wears a protective amulet the child will not die.[24]

Plaskow's modern midrash picks up the story after Lilith leaves the garden. God creates a second companion, Eve, from Adam's side. Eventually Eve sees that Adam identifies himself more and more with God, both being male, to the point that even God is uncomfortable. Meanwhile Lilith tries to rejoin the human community. Adam fends her off, but Eve gets a glimpse of her and sees that she is a woman like herself. Eventually Eve and Lilith meet and begin to share their stories. God and Adam are puzzled about what this might mean. The midrash concludes with Eve and Lilith returning to the garden, bursting with possibilities, ready to build it together.[25]

Both Lilith midrashim speak to the issue of equality between women and men. In the medieval version Lilith is transformed into a demon and poses a menacing danger to the human community. Survival of the next generation is dependent on newborns wearing a protective amulet. In her failure to submit to Adam she serves as a warning to women who question patriarchal authority. In Plaskow's version, when the two women meet and converse they discover how much they have in common. It is this commonality that gives them strength for the task of remaking the world.

Plaskow's midrash articulated the consciousness-raising and strategizing that occurred among the members of her group. It served as an initial model for feminist scholarship in that it highlighted androcentric themes in the fundamental myth of origins common to Judaism and Christianity. It raised questions about whether patriarchy was the intended ordering of society and what consequences result.

While Plaskow's work emphasizes the creation of new feminist theologies, Phyllis Trible emphasizes biblical interpretation as primary to the creation of theology. Trible reads biblical narratives through the lens of feminist thought. She seeks to highlight biblical passages concerning women, with the intention that they can initiate new and more inclusive theologies within religious institutions. Trible's analysis of the Yahwist creation narrative in Gen 2:4b–3:24 has generated nearly twenty-five years of support, critique, and controversy.[26]

---

[24] For a translation of the Lilith midrash see Rosemary Radford Ruether, *Womanguides: Reading Toward a Feminist Theology* (Boston: Beacon, 1985) 71.

[25] Plaskow, "The Coming of Lilith," 206.

[26] Phyllis Trible, "A Love Story Gone Awry" in her *God and the Rhetoric of Sexuality* (Philadelphia: Fortress, 1978) 72–143.

Trible uses a method called "rhetorical criticism," which investigates various ways words are used in a literary unit of text. The technique described in Chapter One for close reading of a narrative facilitates a rhetorical analysis. Trible highlights key words, focusing on repetition, parallel structure, and word plays that show how those words relate to the overall structure of a narrative. She notes that the word *ha'adam* ("humankind" in the *NRSV*) in Gen 1:27 signifies a being from which God creates male and female. "So God created humankind in his image, in the image of God he created them; male and female he created them." In this account the simultaneous creation of woman and man precludes an interpretation claiming that the woman is derived from the man and therefore subservient to him. Using Gen 1:27 as a backdrop, Trible claims that the *'adam* (the human creature formed from the earth) in Gen 2:7 was without sex but contained the potential for sexual differentiation. When God takes the rib of the *'adam* and fashions it into woman, two sexual creatures are formed. Thus men and women are created simultaneously in both the Priestly and Yahwist narratives. Such an interpretation is meant to deny superiority of one sex (male) over the other (female) in both creation narratives.

In Gen 3:6 Trible notes that it is the woman who takes the fruit from the forbidden tree, eats of it, and gives it to her man who is with her, whereupon he also eats. This text indicts both the man and the woman in the act of disobedience, with no mention of the woman tempting the man. The judgment that follows states that the woman will have increased pain in childbearing. Her desire will be for her husband, though what that phrase means is ambiguous. She will also be subject to her husband (Gen 3:16). For his part in the act, the man will be forced to engage in hard work to obtain food from the earth. Trible regards these judgments as direct consequences of the actions of the man and the woman.

Trible's work exposes the ways in which Genesis 2 and 3 have been used to keep women in subordinate positions, but it does not deal with the extent to which patriarchy is embedded in both the Bible itself and in religious institutions.[27] Trible assumes that the equality between the man and the woman found in Gen 1:27 is God's intent for humanity. This is a programmatic reading of Genesis 2–3. The assumption gives precedence to one text over another, based on a belief that the Bible as a whole is liberating.

---

[27] For a critique of Trible's work see Pamela Milne, "Toward Feminist Companionship: The Future of Feminist Biblical Studies and Feminism," in Athalya Brenner and Carole Fontaine, eds., *A Feminist Companion to Reading the Bible: Approaches, Methods and Strategies* (Sheffield: Sheffield Academic Press, 1997) 39–60, and Judith Ochshorn, *The Female Experience and the Nature of the Divine* (Bloomington: Indiana University Press, 1981).

Esther Fuchs claims that Phyllis Trible romanticizes Genesis 1–3 in her assumption that the text is intended to be egalitarian. Fuchs maintains instead that Eve is portrayed as morally inferior to Adam and thus serves as a negative prototype for women in the Bible and in society.[28] Eve's moral inferiority is due solely to her action of offering the fruit from the forbidden tree to Adam. Some interpreters claim that Eve's secondary status and her absence when the original command not to eat the fruit was given serve to lessen her guilt. For Fuchs the punishment given to Eve comes about solely because she took the fruit and ate it and gave it to her husband. She is the agent of Adam's downfall. She is punished with greater pain in childbirth, desire for her husband, and subordination to him. Fuchs notes that the political agenda behind this text is precisely that a woman belongs to a man, that her duty is to produce his children, and that she is to accept his authority. In contrast to Trible, Fuchs does not feel a need to rehabilitate the text. While Fuchs' interpretation is not likely to be quoted in liturgical settings, it does raise serious questions about the pervasiveness of patriarchy in religion and society.

Carol Meyers' interpretation of Genesis 3 is based on her sociohistorical study of Israel before the monarchy. In Chapter One we discussed her view that the definition of patriarchy used by feminists today may not apply to the setting of subsistence agriculture in Israel before 1000 B.C.E. As new social scientific studies inform biblical studies, scholars are even more aware of the impact of ancient culture on texts. The task of identifying sex roles in the ancient world is further complicated when writers from a later period, such as during the monarchy, edit the texts. A more urban social structure is evident during the monarchical period, when women were no longer as involved in subsistence tasks. In Meyers' understanding of Genesis 3 the judgment given to Eve is not a punishment but rather a statement of the reality of the existing hardships for women in premonarchical Israel.[29] Meyers translates Gen 3:16:

> I will greatly increase your work *('tsb)* and your pregnancies.
> (Along) with toil *('tsb)* you shall give birth to children.
> To your man is your desire,
> and he shall predominate over you.

[28] Esther Fuchs, *Sexual Politics in the Biblical Narrative: Reading the Hebrew Bible as a Woman* (Sheffield: Sheffield Academic Press, 2000) 175.

[29] Carol L. Meyers, "Gender Roles and Genesis 3:16 Revisited," in Athalya Brenner, ed., *A Feminist Companion to Genesis* (Sheffield: Sheffield Academic Press, 1997) 130.

In her translation Meyers notes two roles for women. Women produce goods for subsistence living and they bear children. Because of the hardships of the time, women will need to produce more goods and have more children to insure the survival of the household.

Most other translations of Gen 3:16 are similar to the *NRSV,* which reads:

> I will greatly increase your pangs in childbearing;
> in pain you shall bring forth children,
> yet your desire shall be for your husband,
> and he shall rule over you.

This translation emphasizes that it is the woman's pain that will increase, not the number of her pregnancies.

Meyers notes that the Hebrew root '*tsb* is used twice in Gen 3:16 in the divine statement to the woman. The same Hebrew root occurs in Gen 3:17 to speak of the increased toil that the man will encounter in order to grow food. Therefore, the sociological setting is calling for an increased population and harder work. While the man will have to work harder at making the inhospitable, arid ground productive, the woman will have to produce more children and work harder at her tasks. Meyers does not support the notion that the text refers to increased pain in childbirth.

Meyers offers a more sympathetic reading of the phrase "your desire shall be for your man" than do other interpreters. Instead of the idea that the woman's desire will not be equally reciprocated, Meyers suggests that there is a relationship between the woman and the man that goes beyond the sexual process of reproduction. She proposes that while reproduction is necessary, the use of the root *tsqh,* translated "desire," parallels the only other use of the root in Song 7:10: "I am my beloved's and his desire is for me." "Desire" refers to a relationship that transcends merely bearing children.

In the last phrase, "and he shall rule over you," Meyers claims that the man's share of the subsistence work will still be greater than that of the woman. The Hebrew root *(msl)* used in this passage is associated with wise rule rather than autocratic rule. The man will predominate in this work rather than rule like a king over a subject.

Phyllis Bird is concerned about the traditional view held by many that Eve is responsible for the act of disobedience in the garden and is to blame for the subsequent "fall" of humankind. She uses Meyers' interpretation of Genesis 3 in her own discussion of the relationship between Genesis 3 and the Christian doctrine of original sin.[30] She also agrees with Meyers that it is the economic and social circumstances of early Israel that lie behind the injunction to Eve in Gen 3:16. Bird echoes Trible in attributing the act of disobedience to both the woman and the man; therefore the woman is not solely responsible for bringing sin and death into the world.

It is instructive at this point to discuss what is meant by the concept of "original sin." In Christianity, "original sin" refers to the sin of the first humans and the subsequent fallen condition of all humanity. It was not until the third or second century B.C.E. that we know of Jews living in Greek culture began to ask questions about the origin of evil in the world. The narrative in Genesis 2 and 3 became a way of reflecting on the origin of evil. Early evidence for this is found in the book of Sirach, which dates to 180 B.C.E. and was later incorporated into the Apocrypha. Sirach 25:24 states: "From a woman sin had its beginning, and because of her we all die." Sirach is a Jewish writing, but Christianity (in the first four centuries of the Common Era) would develop the idea that sin is passed along through sexual intercourse from one generation to the next. Unfortunately, the stigma of blame attached to Eve, and in some cases to all women, has prevailed through the centuries. More than any other text, Genesis 2–3 has been used to justify the subordinate status of women and misogyny.

In her desire to become wise, the woman in Genesis 3 is attracted to the fruit of the forbidden tree. It would seem that knowledge of good and evil is fundamental to functioning in the world. The wisdom she desired becomes shame and alienation from God and Adam. If that were not enough, more punishments follow. However, the punishments meted out to Adam and Eve do not relate to their crime but to the nature of their roles as man and woman.[31] For Bird there is no hierarchy of punishments. They will each experience pain in their labor and estrangement. Both the man and the woman responded to temptation: she to a desire for knowledge and he in his silent acquiescence. Both chose to disobey the voice of God.

Bird asserts that the narrative in Genesis 2 and 3 does not describe how sin came into the world. Instead it shows that sin arises solely out of human volition and is not a part of creation. While the Yahwist narrative acknowledges the hardships, alienation, and limits placed on human life, it also recognizes that this was not always the case.[32] Life was meant to be as

---

[30] Phyllis Bird, "Genesis 3 in Modern Biblical Scholarship," in her *Missing Persons and Mistaken Identities: Women and Gender in Ancient Israel* (Minneapolis: Fortress, 1997) 174.
[31] Ibid. 190.
[32] Ibid. 178.

it was portrayed prior to the act of disobedience. The narrative speaks of the transformation from the world of origins to the world of reality. If the Genesis narrative is read in light of this wider framework, then blaming the woman for sin undermines the broader task of reclaiming the original unity and equality in Gen 1:27.

Our consideration of the views of five feminist scholars reveals a variety of approaches, methods, and goals under the umbrella of feminist interpretation. For some, like Esther Fuchs, the story's patriarchal stamp makes it irredeemable. Carol Meyers defuses the potency of the text by claiming that women's work and pregnancies will increase as needed for the survival of the community rather than that women's pain in childbirth will increase. Phyllis Trible finds hope rooted in a belief in the ultimate good news of the biblical message. According to Gen 1:27, God created man and woman simultaneously; therefore they are equal. Trible reads the more problematic story in Genesis 2–3 to say the same thing. However, a nagging question remains. Did the biblical authors embrace this message of equality? Fuchs would answer with a resounding "no." In her analysis it is evident that Eve is the villain, or at least such was the assumption of the authors. Phyllis Bird recognizes that this text has fueled the fire of the doctrine of original sin by placing undue blame on women and procreation for the presence of sin in the world. What are the alternatives? Before we throw up our hands, let us recall Judith Plaskow. According to her we should share our experiences, wrestle with various interpretations, and listen to each other. We can retell the story from different points of view and then, like Eve and Lilith, return to the garden ready to renew it.

## Goals of Feminist Interpretation of the Bible

According to Elisabeth Schüssler Fiorenza the task of feminist interpretation is to challenge traditional interpretations of the Bible that support patriarchal structures within institutional religion. The ultimate goal is to bring about social-political change.[33] Traditional hierarchical, or top-down, interpretations that produce theologies of dominance must be replaced with a process that speaks for the oppressed. Feminist scholars must learn from those struggling for change and present that conversation in academic and social settings. Instead of merely imposing their views on those outside of academia, they should actively advocate for change. The task is a radical one. It is both deconstructive and (re)constructive in that it calls for

---

[33] Schüssler Fiorenza, *Wisdom Ways*, 89.

a reassessment of those beliefs and practices that work against liberation and envisions new theologies and structures that mediate justice.[34]

## Summary

In this chapter we have introduced and illustrated various forms of feminist biblical interpretation. We have followed the feminist inquiry into texts that have served to maintain the subordination of women in patriarchal society for millennia. In Chapter Five we will examine the story of Jephthah's daughter from this perspective, citing various scholars. Our ultimate goal is to discern the values the feminists and the rabbis bring to their interpretations. At this point we will return to the medieval world and allow the rabbis to comment on Jephthah's daughter.

[34] Ibid. 93.

# CHAPTER FOUR

## *The Rabbis Speak*

Let us imagine a conversation between the early and medieval rabbis and feminist writers of modern times. What could they possibly have to say to each other about Jephthah's daughter? Are the concerns of the rabbis at all related to the concerns of the feminists, or is each group stereotypically bound by its own time or its own rhetoric? In this chapter we will present the issues raised by the rabbis and show how their discussion of the narrative of Jephthah's daughter relates to concerns raised by feminist thinkers.

### What Are the Rabbinical Sources?

The commentaries and midrash to be examined in this section date from the first through the thirteenth centuries C.E. The earliest sources in this collection are the anonymous work of Pseudo-Philo and *The Antiquities of the Jews,* written by Josephus, a Jew who was supported by the Romans after they destroyed Jerusalem in 70 C.E. Josephus rewrites the history of Israel from creation to Roman times, and his goal is to portray Jews as an honorable people with a rich tradition. In retelling the story of Jephthah, Josephus claims that Jephthah's sacrifice was not acceptable to God. Pseudo-Philo, who retells the history of Israel from Adam to David, reflects thinking in Palestinian synagogues at the beginning of Christianity. As noted in Chapter Two, Pseudo-Philo contains an elaborate midrash on Jephthah's daughter.

Another major source of Jewish midrash is *Midrash Rabbah.* This collection contains midrash for all five books of the Torah as well as Song of Songs, Lamentations, Ecclesiastes, Ruth, and Esther. These writings date from the fourth to the twelfth centuries.[1] Another form of midrash is found in targums, which are translations of the Hebrew Tanakh into Aramaic, the vernacular language of the Jews. The targums contain internal interpretations added by the translators. Of interest to our study is a later targum, *Targum Jonathan of the Former Prophets,* dated from the seventh to the ninth century.[2] We will also cite texts from the third-century Mishnah and the Talmud, the sixth-century commentary on the Mishnah. Rounding out rabbinic commentary on Jephthah's daughter are midrashim found in *Tanhuma Be-hukkotai* (ninth-tenth century), *Alphabet Ben Sira* (eleventh century), and the writings of David Kimhi (thirteenth century).

Several of these collections repeat midrash from other sources with some variation. In this work we will not attempt to trace the sources or to give a detailed comparison of each version. Instead, we will be concerned with the content of the midrash as it pertains to Judges 11.[3]

## Rabbinic Concerns Regarding Jephthah and His Daughter

Overall, the rabbis have very little patience with Jephthah for making and carrying out his vow. They point out that Jephthah had alternatives other than sacrificing his daughter. Moreover, they endow the daughter with a name, human emotion, wisdom, compassion, and a capacity to seek help for herself. In the following section we will imagine questions the rabbis brought to the narrative silences of the text and then present their responses to those questions, using their own words as they have come down in the midrash.

### Did Jephthah's Background Foreshadow His Success or Failure as a Judge?

In the opening verses of Judges 11 we are told that Jephthah is a son of a harlot and half-brother of legitimate sons. He leaves home and goes raiding with outlaws. The rabbis conclude that his background foreshadows his failure as a judge. In the Babylonian Talmud tractate *b. Baba Qamma* 92b they quote Judg 11:3, "and there gathered themselves to Jephthah idle

---

[1] Dates for collections of midrash are taken from Raphael Patai, ed., *Gates to the Old City: A Book of Jewish Legends* (Northvale, NJ: Jason Aronson, 1980) 260.

[2] *Targum Jonathan of the Former Prophets*, trans. Daniel J. Harrington and Anthony J. Saldarini (Wilmington: Michael Glazier, 1987). For a discussion of the date see Jacob Neusner, *Introduction to Rabbinic Literature* (New York: Doubleday, 1994) 618.

[3] See Appendix for texts of the midrash discussed in this chapter.

men, and they went out with him." Affixed to this quotation is an analogy, "a bad date palm will make its way to a grove of barren trees." The Mishnah is also quoted: "Anything joined to what is susceptible to uncleanness is itself susceptible to uncleanness" (*m. Kelim* 12:2). The rabbis conclude that Jephthah's failure can be traced back to his choice of unsuitable companions. Note that the midrash does not condemn Jephthah's mother for being a harlot. Likewise, in the biblical story, her status is not condemned nor considered a cause for Jephthah's failure. Instead, the passage blames Jephthah for his choice of companions and carries a warning that bad behavior is contagious.

## Did Jephthah Give Thought to the Way He Phrased His Vow?

Jephthah vows that if God will grant him victory over the Ammonites he will offer whoever comes forth from his house as a sacrifice to God. In *Gen. Rab.* 60.3 the rabbis discuss proper and improper ways of requesting favors from God because God can, in turn, respond to requests in proper and improper ways. The four examples of Eliezer, Caleb, Saul, and Jephthah are cited. All ask God for a favor in an improper way. Despite their rashness, Eliezer, Caleb, and Saul receive a "proper" or desired outcome, but Jephthah receives an "improper" or undesirable outcome.

Eliezer, Abraham's servant, is sent to find a wife for Isaac. He prays, "Let the maiden to whom I shall say, 'Pray let down your jar that I may drink,' that she will say 'Drink, and I will water your camels.'" This is to be a sign that this woman is to be Isaac's wife. Eliezer acted rashly in that he did not consider what would have been the outcome if the woman had been a slave. Fortunately for him, the woman was Rebecca. This "improper" request could have resulted in a slave being the one to wed Isaac.

Similarly, Caleb promises that whoever captures Kiriath Sepher will be granted his daughter, Achsah, as a wife. But what if the warrior had been a slave? Fortunately the valiant Othniel is a proper choice and he marries Achsah.

In like manner, according to the midrash, when Saul is looking for someone to slay the giant Goliath he agrees to grant the victor his daughter as a wife. As in the other two cases, the improper outcome would be that the hero would be a slave. However, the suitable choice is David, who successfully slays Goliath.

By contrast, Jephthah's improper request does not result in a proper outcome. In this case God responds to Jephthah's vow by asking, "If a camel or an ass or a dog should come forth from your house, would you then offer him up as a burnt offering before me?" These animals were considered unclean and therefore could not be offered as a sacrifice. In this midrash God is credited with having Jephthah's daughter come forth from the house. The daughter, like the unclean animals, is not an acceptable sacrifice, not because she is unclean but because she is a human being. In this midrash Jephthah is brought low. By the logic of the midrash the other fathers (Eliezer representing Abraham) might have had to accept a social inferior as their child's marriage partner, but Jephthah is punished more severely because he will lose his daughter and hence any potential offspring.

Embedded in the *Genesis Rabbah* midrash is an implied social hierarchy. A slave is inferior to a non-slave. Social hierarchy is more evident in another version of this midrash in *Lev. Rab.* 37:4. In this version Eliezer's request might result in the emergence of a Canaanite, a slave-girl, or a harlot. In Caleb's case a Canaanite, a bastard, or a slave might be the victor. In Saul's case an Ammonite, a bastard, or a slave might have been the one to slay Goliath. In Jephthah's case, since a camel, ass, or dog is declared an improper choice, readers may be shocked that God is credited with bringing out Jephthah's daughter. Clearly she does not represent one of the improper social groupings. She shares the social status of Rebecca, Othniel, and David. Thus Jephthah is shamed. Even if all four men make improper requests, Jephthah is the one who suffers. The question remains why Jephthah was punished in this manner and why the daughter paid the ultimate price.

A third version of this midrash, found in *b. Ta'anit* 4a, claims that Jephthah was fortunate that his daughter came out to meet him. This midrash quotes Jer. 8:22: "[I]s there no balm in Gilead? Is there no physician there?" It offers answers to the dilemma about why God chose the daughter to come out of the house. Yes, Jephthah is shamed, but according to the midrash he has alternatives to sacrificing his daughter.

## What Alternatives Did Jephthah Have?

Did Jephthah really have to sacrifice his daughter to fulfill his vow? Was there another way to satisfy his obligation? In *Gen. Rab.* 60.3 the rabbis discuss what constitutes an acceptable sacrifice. They refer to a text from the Mishnah stating that an unclean or blemished animal was not acceptable. One must sell the unclean or blemished animal and use the proceeds to buy an appropriate animal (*m. Temurah* 5.6). According to this text Jephthah could have paid a redemption price for his daughter and substituted another animal for the sacrifice. It appears that Jephthah is either ignorant of the law or unwilling to explore alternatives.

The rabbis present differing opinions as to whether Jephthah was legally responsible for keeping his vow. One opinion states that Jephthah should have redeemed his daughter instead of offering her as a sacrifice. Another opinion states that legally Jephthah was not even responsible for the redemption payment, since the vow was invalid from the outset (*Gen. Rab.* 60.3).

### Why Did Jephthah Fail to Consult with a Priest or an Official?

The biblical account may lead us to believe that the entire sequence of events involves only the father and the daughter. The reader may wonder if other religious or civil authorities could have been consulted. The rabbis explore the issue by positing a role for the priest Phinehas (*Gen. Rab.* 60.3, *Lev. Rab.* 37:4, *Tan. B.* 5.7). This midrash hinges on two proud men who will not condescend to visit each other: "Phinehas said, 'Lo, he needs me, and should I go to him? And not only so, but I am high priest and the son of a high priest, and should I go to an ordinary person?' Jephthah said, 'I am the head of the rulers of Israel, and should I go to Phinehas?'"

The dilemma ends with the statement that because of the stubbornness of both men the girl perished. A proverb is added: "Between the midwife and the woman in travail, the poor woman's baby is going to die." According to another source, if Jephthah had inquired of Phinehas, Jephthah could have redeemed his daughter in blood by offering an appropriate animal sacrifice (*Tg. Neb.* Judg 11:39).

According to the midrash, Jephthah could have consulted Phinehas regarding release from his vow, and it appears that Phinehas knew of Jephthah's predicament but offered no help. Both men chose to cling to their own pride of position over the needs of the daughter.

### What Was Jephthah's Daughter's Name?

Pseudo-Philo often gives names to nameless characters in the Bible. In Pseudo-Philo 40 Jephthah's daughter is named Seila. The Hebrew root *š'l* means "ask," and Seila is the one "asked for" or "requested." Upon seeing her come from the house, Jephthah says that she was rightly named since she asked to be a sacrifice. This explanation seeks to justify her fate by the name given her at birth.[4]

---

[4] James H. Charlesworth, *The Old Testament Pseudepigrapha* (Garden City, NY: Doubleday, 1985) 2:353.

## What Conversation Took Place Between Father and Daughter When Jephthah Returned?

Pseudo-Philo heightens the emotional exchange between Jephthah and his daughter when he returns from battle. Pseudo-Philo 40:1 notes that a group of women comes out to meet Jephthah in song and dance, but Seila is the first to emerge. Upon seeing her, Jephthah grows faint. His immediate response is to justify the situation by linking her name, "asked for," to the catastrophic events that are bound to follow. He asks, "Who will put my heart in the balance and my soul on the scale? I will stand by and see which will win out, whether it is the rejoicing that has occurred or the sadness that befalls me." He is sure that his vow cannot be taken back. His lament is more concerned with his own sorrow than with his daughter's impending death. It is all about him.

At this point Seila responds, "Who is it who would be sad in death, seeing the people freed?" (Ps.-Philo 40:2). She puts the national interests above her own life. She recalls that when Abraham offered Isaac, "Abraham rejoiced and Isaac gladly gave consent to being sacrificed."[5] The drama escalates as she worries about whether she will be an acceptable sacrifice. "If I do not offer myself willingly for sacrifice, I fear that my death would not be acceptable or I would die in vain" (Ps.-Philo 40:3). Her concern over the purity of the sacrifice leads her to deny the physical reality of what is to befall her.

In the biblical story both father and daughter suffer and both care deeply for each other. Jephthah tears his clothes in mourning when his daughter emerges from his house. His daughter acknowledges his dilemma and agrees to the stipulation of his vow. However, neither one can envision alternatives. The father will keep his word at all cost. The daughter will go to her death bravely as a martyr or a witness to her father's vow. At this point in the narrative neither considers that within their tradition there might be a solution to the problem.

## What Alternatives Did the Daughter Have?

In the biblical account it appears that once Jephthah's daughter consents to being sacrificed there is no other option for her. Nevertheless, she negotiates a two-month respite to spend time with her friends. While the biblical version says nothing about what the women did during the two months, the rabbis fill in the blanks, speculating that she actively sought help through appropriate channels, something her father was too proud to do.

[5] The midrash on Abraham and Isaac is found in Pseudo-Philo 32:2-4.

Some of the rabbis postulate that the daughter did not go to the mountains, but sought help for herself. Their argument is based on the use of two words in the narrative: "go down," *yrd* in Hebrew, and "mountains," *hr* in Hebrew. Does the reference to "mountains" in Judg 11:37 literally mean mountains, or does it mean something else? The daughter says "Grant me two months, so that I may go and *yrd* on the mountains." The Hebrew root *yrd* can mean to come, go down, or wander. If *yrd* means to go down, then the text reads that she went down to the mountains instead of the usual *ʿlh,* to go up to the mountains. An example of going down to the mountains is found in Exod 19:20. When the LORD descended *(yrd)* to the top of Mount Sinai, the LORD summoned Moses to the top of the mountain, and Moses went up *(ʿlh)*. One can only go down to the mountains if one is imagined as above the mountains. Moses, positioned below, goes up. The meaning of *yrd* creates a narrative silence that the rabbis address. Interestingly, the *NRSV* avoids this dilemma by translating *yrd* as "to wander." The daughter goes and wanders on the mountains.

If one translates *yrd* as "to go down," then perhaps "the mountains" stand for something other than a physical landform. According to *Exod. Rab.* 15:4, "mountains" can refer to ancestors or to elders. For example, a rabbi quotes Mic 6:2, "Hear, O mountains, the LORD's controversy. Rise, plead your case before the mountains." Here "mountains" is said to refer to elders. *Exodus Rabbah* quotes Judg 11:37 as "that I may go down upon the mountains." The rabbis ask, " Did Jephthah's daughter go upon the mountains? No, she went to the elders to prove to them that she was a pure virgin" (*Exod. Rab.* 15:4). The point the rabbis are making is that the daughter did not go to the mountains but consulted the elders about her virginity. The meaning of virginity will be discussed by feminist interpreters.

According to Ps.-Philo 40:4, Seila, accompanied by her companions, went to the wise men of the people, but no one could respond to her. Pseudo-Philo offers the explanation that God was responsible for their lack of response so that God's plan would not be curtailed. "The Lord . . . said, 'Behold now I have shut up the tongue of the wise men of my people for this generation so that they cannot respond to the daughter of Jephthah, in order that my word be fulfilled and my plan that I thought out not be foiled" (Ps.-Philo 40:4). God affirms the sacrifice and says that her death will be precious in God's sight. This seemingly heartless portrayal of God might be lessened if God did this to show that the vow was invalid. According to Lev 27:1-8 the price of redemption is clearly stipulated. Perhaps God wanted to alert Jephthah to the severity of his actions. If this is the case, then God could have chosen to spare the daughter.

According to these midrashim both Jephthah and his daughter had access to structures in their tradition that could address their plight. Though the structures were available, the officials failed them. The priest Phinehas was a poor judicial representative who was too proud to consult with Jephthah. The elders to whom the daughter appealed are helpless to act. Interestingly, the midrash shows that a woman could approach a judicial body; yet, in this case, she did not receive a sympathetic hearing or even a judgment.

## If the Women Went to the Mountains, What Did They Do There?

While the prose portion of Pseudo-Philo 40 emphasizes Seila's willingness to be a martyr, the author inserts a poem that she speaks, mourning her unfulfilled life as a woman. The poem is rich in imagery, detailing wedding preparations of the day. In this poem Seila is not speaking pious platitudes; she is a real flesh-and-blood young woman who wants to have a wedding. It sounds as if wedding preparations have already begun, making her fate all the more tragic.

Seila's poem lends itself to symmetrical thematic analysis in which units of the poem can be arranged to show a formal balancing of themes and expose a central unit. This particular poem can be diagramed as A-B-C-D-C'-B'-A' in the pattern of concentric reverse symmetry.[6] The central element in this arrangement, labeled D, reveals that Seila's most intimate words are addressed to her mother. (Note that Seila's mother does not appear in the biblical narrative or in any other midrash.) Seila laments:

A Hear, you mountains, my lamentation;
and pay attention, you hills, to the tears of my eyes;
and be witness, you rocks, of the weeping of my soul.
B Behold how I am put to the test!
But not in vain will my life be taken away.
May my words go forth in the heavens,
and my tears be written in the firmament!
That a father did not refuse the daughter, whom he had sworn to sacrifice,
that a ruler granted that his only daughter be promised for sacrifice.

---

[6] For a discussion of reverse symmetry see Jerome T. Walsh, *Style and Structure in Biblical Hebrew Narrative* (Collegeville: Liturgical Press, 2001) 13–34.

C  But I have not made good on my marriage chamber,
   and I have not retrieved my wedding garlands.
   For I have not been clothed in splendor while sitting in my
      woman's chamber.
   And I have not used the sweet-smelling ointment.
   And my soul has not rejoiced in the oil of anointing that has been
      prepared for me.

D  O Mother, in vain have you borne your only daughter,
   because Sheol has become my bridal chamber,
   And on earth there is only my woman's chamber.

C' And may all the blend of oil that you have prepared for me be
      poured out,
   and the white robe that my mother has woven, the moth will eat it.
   And the crown of flowers that my nurse plaited for me for the
      festival, may it wither up;
   And the coverlet that she wove of hyacinth and purple in my
      woman's chamber,
   may the worm devour it.

B' And may my virgin companions tell of me in sorrow and weep for
      me through the days.

A' You trees, bow down your branches and weep over my youth,
   You beasts of the forests, come and bewail my virginity,
   for my years have been cut off and the time of my life grown old
      in darkness.

A concentric reverse symmetry grid reveals a progression of Seila's grief. In the verse labeled A Seila calls the vast reaches of nature to witness her lamentation. In A', nature responds as trees bow down and the beasts lament. Element B tells of the father's promise to sacrifice his daughter. No circumstances are mentioned, only that she will be a sacrifice. There is no mention of the father's grief. B' replaces the father with the testimony and grief of the women friends. Element C mentions her wedding garlands, her woman's chamber, ointments, and an anointing awaiting her. C' sees the disintegration of all the finery of the preparations. Fabric will rot, flowers will wither, and worms will devour the coverlet. What was not quite hers to begin with will disintegrate unused. The heart of this poem is the relationship between mother and daughter. In D, Seila consoles her mother who has borne a daughter in futility. Seila's fate is Sheol, the place of separation and isolation.

Although this poem is a lament, it does not contain the language of martyrdom. There is no mention of military interests. There is minimal attention given to Jephthah; he is only the cause of her plight. While the poem appears in a larger work authored by men, one has to wonder if it was a part of a women's tradition, perhaps even a commemoration similar to the annual gathering of the daughters of Israel mentioned in Judg 11:40. The poem speaks of the world of women as friends, mourners, and mothers.[7]

## Did Jephthah's Daughter Go Silently to Her Death?

In the biblical account, one brief sentence is allotted to the daughter's death. "She returned to her father and he did with her according to the vow he had made." According to *Tanhuma B.* the daughter protested her death, citing examples from the Tanakh to support her case. As Jephthah is about to offer her up, she pleads, "My father, my father, I came out to meet you full of joy, and now you are about to slaughter me. Is it written in the Torah that Israel should offer the lives of their children upon the altar?" Jephthah replies, "My daughter, I made a vow." She reminds him that Jacob also made a vow. He vowed to give God one tenth of what God had given to him. God gave Jacob twelve sons, and yet Jacob did not offer even one of them on the altar. In addition, she reminds her father that Hannah vowed to give her son to God for his entire life, but not as a sacrifice. Jephthah is not persuaded by her arguments. He slaughters her on the altar before the Holy One. The Holy Spirit cries out in anguish, "Have I ever asked you to offer living souls to me? I commanded not, nor spoke it, neither came it into my mind" (*Tanh.B.* 5.7).

The daughter argues with her father in the style of the rabbis themselves. She cites biblical examples of Jacob and Hannah, reinterpreting their actions in light of her own situation. The Jacob and Hannah narratives say nothing about human sacrifice. The daughter of the midrash draws these notable and revered characters into her story as witnesses to her cause. Jephthah's act flouts tradition and the very spirit of God as expressed in the Tanakh.

## Did Anyone Pay for Not Upholding Justice?

While there appears to be no justice for Jephthah's daughter, the rabbis find a rather morbid justice for Jephthah and Phinehas. The rabbis envision

---

[7] For another treatment of this poem see Barbara B. Miller, "Women, Death, and Mourning in the Ancient Eastern Mediterranean World" (Ph.D. diss., University of Michigan–Ann Arbor: University Microfilms International, 1994) 200–208.

a graphic justice for Jephthah. In the biblical story, after sacrificing his daughter Jephthah fails in negotiations with the Ephraimites. Civil war follows, and forty-two thousand from the tribe of Ephraim are killed (Judg 12:1-6). Jephthah's life spirals downward, and he judges Israel for only six years. It appears that the rabbis need to find a memorable punishment to describe their frustration with this leader of Israel. According to Judg 12:7 Jephthah died and was buried in the *cities* of Gilead rather than in one city. The midrash claims that Jephthah's limbs fell off, limb by limb, and he was buried in many places (*Gen. Rab.* 60.3, *Lev. Rab.* 37:4; *Eccl. Rab.* 10:15).

The same rabbis claim that the Holy Spirit departed from Phinehas. This is based on 1 Chr 9:20: "And Phinehas son of Eleazar was chief over them in former times; the LORD was with him." The midrash makes it clear that while the Holy Spirit was with Phinehas in the past, that was no longer the case. Phinehas, like Saul, suffers the loss of the Spirit of the LORD. The assurance of God's presence is no longer available to him. While there are no details describing how Phinehas suffered, one is reminded of Saul's personal degradation, insanity, and eventual suicide.

## *What Is the Significance of the Women's Four-Day Ritual?*

Rabbinic midrash records a legend that attempts to understand the significance of the number four in the four-day tradition that developed after the daughter's death. In this legend the number four was connected with the four turnings of the sun in the vernal and autumnal equinoxes and the summer and winter solstices. It was said that drops of blood poisoned water on the four turnings of the sun. Each of the poisonings was linked to a biblical narrative. At the vernal equinox God turned the waters of Egypt into blood, so that every year a drop of blood was thrown into the water to poison it. At the summer solstice, when Moses smote the rock and blood came forth, every year a drop of blood was thrown into the water. At the vernal equinox, when Abraham stretched out his hand to slay Isaac and the knife began to bleed, a drop of blood was thrown into the water. Finally, at the winter solstice, when Jephthah offered his daughter as a sacrifice and his knife began to bleed, a drop of blood was thrown into the water. At the turning of the sun on these four days the maidens of Israel went to lament Jephthah's daughter.[8] In the biblical versions of these accounts blood acts as a poisoning agent only during the plagues of Egypt. The other three references imagine blood at the sacrifice of Isaac, the smiting of the rock,

---

[8] *Alphabet of Ben Sira* 4a-4b, quoted in Louis Ginzberg, *The Legends of the Jews* (Philadelphia: Jewish Publication Society of America, 1913) 4:110 n. 109.

and slaying of Jephthah's daughter. This legend may represent an attempt to link mourning rituals to pagan rites. Aside from this midrash there seems to be no other reference to the ritual of the women mourning Jephthah's daughter.

## How Does the Midrash Evaluate Jephthah?

For the most part the reader or hearer of the midrash is left to evaluate Jephthah on the basis of the stories presented. The first-century Jewish historian Josephus clearly states his opinion, however.[9] Although he applauds Jephthah's military efforts that secured freedom for his people after eighteen years of oppression, he claims that once Jephthah returns home his life suffers a reversal because the burnt offering of a child was not in accordance with the law and was not acceptable to God. Josephus adds that Jephthah was shortsighted as to the way tradition would remember what he did (*Ant.* 5.7.10).

## What Was God's Reaction?

In the biblical account God plays a minor role in the drama. The Spirit of the LORD comes upon Jephthah, Jephthah makes a vow to the LORD, and the LORD delivers the Ammonites into Jephthah's hand. God then withdraws from the drama. In some of the midrash God is more active. In Pseudo-Philo, God closes the mouths of the wise so that they cannot respond when the daughter seeks their help. The reason given for this is that the plan must be carried out. The daughter's death is said to be precious in God's sight. The image of God set forth in this midrash appears more callous than the withdrawal of God in Judges. One solution to this dilemma is to recognize that by the first century many Jews embraced concepts of judgment and afterlife. The description of Seila's fate is that "she will go away and fall into the bosom of her mothers" (Ps.-Philo 40:4). Note that "to fall into the bosom of her mothers" is unusual. In Gen 15:15 Abraham will go to his fathers in peace *(RSV)*. In Gen 47:30 Jacob will lie down with his fathers *(RSV)*. While this language is similar to the idea of going to one's fathers at death, by the time of Pseudo-Philo ideas about afterlife had changed. One does not merely "sleep" with the ancestors; one is called to account for one's deeds. Elsewhere in Pseudo-Philo this is more explicit:

---

[9] Josephus writes an interpretive history of the Jewish people in *The Antiquities of the Jews*. His writings are not categorized as midrash directly, but they offer interpretation of biblical narratives.

"Let us not mourn over these things that we suffer; but because whatever we ourselves have devised, these will we receive" (Ps.-Philo 44:10). Thus God is free to expose Jephthah's deed and uphold the daughter in the afterlife.

This collection of midrashim portrays God as one who is involved in Israel's history. God designates the correct marriage partners during the patriarchal period, the confederacy, and the monarchy (*Gen. Rab.* 60.3; *Lev. Rab.* 37:4). God shows mercy even when humans implore God improperly, but this is not always the case. God can withdraw God's spirit at will. God requires that humans uphold the law. God can be angry and react with sarcasm, as in the reply about offering an unclean animal as a sacrifice. God also speaks directly, saying human sacrifice is never required (*b.Ta'an.* 4a).

The God of the midrash may not necessarily conform to human expectations. God does not intervene to save the daughter. Human notions of God's justice do not necessarily fit reality. Humans are left to work out their corporate and individual lives. Like the God of the Bible, God will be God and humans will endeavor to understand who God is.

## *Did Jephthah's Daughter Really Die?*

A late midrash, attributed to David Kimhi (also known as Radak) claims that Jephthah's daughter did not die. According to this tradition Jephthah did not kill her because she does not say, "I will mourn for my life," but rather "I will mourn for my virginity." The important difference in the choice of words indicates that she was not sacrificed, but was required to remain a virgin. This is affirmed in Judg 11:39: "She had never slept with a man." According to Kimhi she returned, and Jephthah fulfilled the vow he had made, but not by sacrificing her. Instead, he built her a house and placed her there. The daughter then became a recluse, living apart from the world. Her lifelong virginity was the offering that fulfilled the vow. Kimhi's model for her new lifestyle may well have been medieval Christian nuns living in monasteries.[10]

## What Values Do the Rabbis Bring to Their Interpretation?

One of the goals of this book is for us to discern values in the interpretations of the rabbis, feminists, and writers of modern midrash. These

---

[10] Leila Leah Bronner, *From Eve to Esther: Rabbinic Reconstructions of Biblical Women* (Louisville: Westminster John Knox, 1994) 133. David Marcus, *Jephthah and His Vow* (Lubbock: Texas Tech Press, 1986) 8.

values may be practical or theological or both. On a practical level the rabbis uphold the value of integrity, particularly in one's speech. Let your yes be yes, your no be no. In other words, they remind us to consider carefully what we are willing to commit ourselves to and then to do it. Vows calling upon the name of God are only to be used on rare occasions. Careful speech creates a society of trust in which litigation is the exception rather than the norm.

A second practical value in the midrash is humility. Humility is presented as a contrast to false pride. We see that Jephthah and Phinehas became locked in their own self-importance, and tragedy was the result. The rabbis are concerned with leaders who fail to recognize their own shortcomings and the possible consequences of their arrogance. They teach us a timeless lesson: that leadership requires wisdom and humility.

A dominant theological value in the midrash concerns the complex relationship between human and divine justice. The midrashim illustrate that human attempts to carry out justice are flawed. Societal systems of justice are always imperfect. Someone is likely to suffer, even an innocent party. Yet one is obliged to seek justice through the proper channels.

We may be perplexed that divine justice remains in the shadow in these texts. There is no description of a divine plan. Even when evil acts result in more evil acts, God does not intervene. Yet God is present in the teachings, and humans are to interpret the teachings in the best interest of the community. In *Tanh. B.* 5.7 we read that Jephthah was not a Torah scholar. Jephthah's concept of keeping a vow was wrong, and he, his daughter, and the Ephraimites suffered for it. Was the law concerning the keeping of vows responsible for the daughter's death? No. God's justice is entrusted to human beings, whose responsibility it is to exercise it wisely.

## What Issues Are Not Covered in the Midrash?

As modern readers of midrash we might be struck by the sensitivity the rabbis show toward Jephthah's daughter. They portray her as a Torah scholar, a wise woman, an active seeker of justice, a friend to other women, a woman who seeks to fulfill her expected role as a wife, and a woman who mourns. All of these are honorable roles for a woman within the patriarchal social structure of the ancient and medieval worlds.

A modern feminist reader views the Jephthah narrative within a larger framework. Feminism is concerned with the patriarchal social structure itself and the limitations it places on women. Patriarchy affirms the perpetuation of a male-dominated social structure and is, therefore, the primary target for a feminist critique. The issues raised in this critique are relevant to the empowerment of women today. What does this narrative say of social inequities, abused daughters, motherless daughters, unfulfilled lives, friendship, and ritual innovation? Chapter Five will highlight these issues.

## Summary

In this chapter we have presented medieval rabbinic commentary on the tragic story of Jephthah's daughter. The rabbis wrestle with how to reconcile human behavior within society with changing concepts of God. Their midrash addresses concrete issues of justice and is told in the form of story. The reflections are not overtly philosophical, but practical. In Chapter Six we will explore the values the rabbis bring to these stories.

# CHAPTER FIVE
## The Feminists Speak

One of the early feminist biblical critics from the nineteenth century, Elizabeth Cady Stanton, notes that Jephthah "owns his daughter absolutely, having her life even at his disposal." Stanton is outraged that the daughter's submission and self-sacrifice have been applauded by so many people. She imagines a conversation in which the daughter tells her father, "I will not consent to such a sacrifice. You may sacrifice your own life if you please, but you have no right over mine. Life is to me full of hope and happiness. Better that you die than I, if the God whom you worship is pleased with the sacrifice of human life."[1]

Stanton depicts the daughter as one who can see beyond or outside the patriarchal system of her times. She also questions the notion of a god who requires human sacrifice. Stanton's anger is motivated by her own frustration with institutional religion that has kept women in subservient roles, thereby impeding the women's suffrage movement to which Stanton dedicated her life.

Stanton's treatment of Judges 11 emphasizes two important aspects of feminist criticism. First, she raises an impassioned question that grows out of her personal experience of working for women's equality. She claims that women often work against their own self-interest and thus end up supporting systems that keep them oppressed. Instead, she affirms a radical rejection of religiously sanctioned self-sacrifice as portrayed in Judges 11. Second, in a part of her critique not quoted here Stanton shows evidence of doing some homework on the text. She is aware of the alternate tradition

---

[1] Elizabeth Cady Stanton, *The Woman's Bible* (Boston: Northeastern University Press, 1993) 25.

that the daughter was sequestered rather than killed, and she knows that motherhood was highly valued in ancient Israel. However, by modern standards her research may reflect inadequate information and the methods of her time. Feminist critique now requires far more careful scholarship than she used in *The Woman's Bible*.

## Feminist Concerns Regarding Jephthah's Daughter

In this chapter we will pose questions that feminists bring to the Jephthah text and then present answers found in feminist scholarship. The scholars to be quoted here bring a passionate concern for justice to feminist criticism. Their conclusions vary widely. Some of them remain within the patriarchal structure of Judaism and Christianity while others position themselves on the edge or outside it. They use various methods of biblical criticism including rhetorical, historical, social, and psychological criticism. They share some concerns with Stanton, but they employ more critical exegetical skills in their work.

### Why Does Jephthah's Daughter Have No Name?

Jephthah's daughter is one of the unnamed women in the Bible. She is only identified by her relationship to her father. In her role as daughter she is perfectly obedient, even unto death. J. Cheryl Exum suggests that her name-lessness in the text is related to her inability to function independently. By contrast, if she is given a name she can no longer be kept at a distance.[2] Mieke Bal names the daughter Bat (Hebrew for "daughter").[3] The name stresses her dependence and inequality while acknowledging her as a full character. Bal claims that not naming her in the Bible and in subsequent interpretations violates her worth as an individual. As an unnamed character she is known only as a virgin, a victim, and an obedient daughter. These are the attributes assigned to her in the patriarchal casting of the narrative. Ironically, in spite of her anonymity in the biblical story she is the one who is remembered by the women with an annual ceremony (Judg 11:40).

To some extent anonymity can serve to expose the injustice in patriarchal family life by emphasizing filial language. The use of "daughter"

---

[2] J. Cheryl Exum, *Fragmented Women: Feminist (Sub)versions of Biblical Narratives* (Valley Forge, PA: Trinity Press International, 1993) 176.

[3] Mieke Bal, *Death & Dissymmetry: The Politics of Coherence in the Book of Judges* (Chicago: University of Chicago Press, 1988) 43. Bal transliterates the Hebrew *bat*, or "daughter" in English, as *bath*.

rather than a name underscores the context in which the tragedy occurs. On the other hand, Adele Reinhartz claims that, while Jephthah's daughter fits the role of the obedient daughter, she also challenges that role in two instances. First, she places the responsibility for the tragedy on her father. After he blames her for the calamity she shifts the responsibility back to him saying, "My father, if *you* have opened your mouth to the LORD, do to me according to *your* vow." He alone is the one responsible for her death, and she makes that clear.[4] Second, when she requests the time away with her friends she moves outside of the patriarchal sphere of domestic life to a new sphere inhabited by women. Reinhartz sees her as active on her own behalf within the limitations of her situation. Rather than viewing her namelessness as an indication of her helplessness, Reinhartz sees that her status as a daughter without a name calls attention to the injustices in patriarchal family life. Reinhartz qualifies Bal's argument by noting a broader sociological context.

## Is Jephthah's Daughter a Hero or a Victim?

Tikva Frymer-Kensky makes a case for Jephthah's daughter as a hero, based on her brave decision to honor her father's vow.[5] In so doing, the daughter becomes an archetypal hero whom other young women can admire. She is like other women and yet special in that she was given to God rather than to a man in marriage. A similar literary motif occurs in Euripides' tragedy *Iphigenia* from the fifth century B.C.E. In this drama Agamemnon's daughter, Iphigenia, is planning to marry Achilles. She runs to meet her father, only to discover that she is to be offered as a sacrifice to the goddess Artemis. She agrees to the sacrifice, saying, "If Artemis is minded to take this body, am I, a weak mortal, to thwart the goddess?" Jephthah's daughter, like Iphigenia, is an archetypal daughter whose story could be retold in a ceremony marking the transition for young women at puberty. The young women participating in such a rite of passage might see Jephthah's daughter as an example of piety and devotion as they enter upon their dual role of wife and mother. Frymer-Kensky claims that while they might admire Jephthah's daughter's devotion, they would gain comfort from knowing that her fate was not theirs. However, instead of blind devotion, the story of Jephthah's daughter might create fear and dread among young women, or

---

[4] Adele Reinhartz, *"Why Ask My Name?": Anonymity and Identity in Biblical Narrative* (New York: Oxford University Press, 1998) 120.

[5] Tikva Frymer-Kensky, *Reading the Women of the Bible: A New Interpretation of Their Stories* (New York: Schocken Books, 2002) 114.

she might serve as a warning to young women that such obedience could lead to death.

Jo Ann Hackett does not classify Jephthah's daughter as a hero, yet she points out that the women in the first part of Judges fare better in the various narratives than their male counterparts.[6] For example, Deborah outshines Barak, Yael bests Sisera, the women in Samson's life show him up, and Jephthah's daughter exposes her father's rash vow. Hackett speculates that these narratives might have been preserved and retold in women's rituals similar to the one mentioned in Judg 11:40. While not a hero in the sense that she gains power over her adversary, Jephthah's daughter gains the sympathy of her women friends in the narrative as well as winning over some midrashic writers and modern feminists.

Others see Jephthah's daughter as a victim. Phyllis Trible claims that Jephthah's daughter is a victim of her father's faithless vow.[7] Jephthah already possessed the Spirit of the LORD when he made a vow to offer as a sacrifice whatever came forth first from his house upon his return. It appears that Jephthah did not fully trust the spirit to insure his victory, but made an unnecessary vow as added insurance. Yet others might see his vow as a sign of his faith in the spirit that came upon him. In this view the vow affirms the presence of the spirit.

Trible notes that Jephthah's words of blame overwhelm the daughter who must comply with the vow made to God. When Jephthah sees his daughter, both of them testify to the inviolability of the vow made to God. As the brave victim, she does not pity herself and does not show anger. Trible claims that her death is a premeditated death, a sentence of murder passed upon an innocent victim.[8] The language of the vow frames the daughter's fate. "A vow led to victory; victory produced a victim; the victim died by violence, violence has, in turn, fulfilled the vow."[9] For Trible the tradition that remembers the daughter shifts the focus of the narrative from death to life. Jephthah's daughter becomes a symbol for all courageous daughters of faithless fathers.

Trible was among the first feminist writers to bring to light the narratives of forgotten women who were victims of patriarchal structures. Her

[6] Jo Ann Hackett, "In the Days of Jael: Reclaiming the History of Women in Ancient Israel," in Clarissa W. Atkinson, Constance H. Buchanan, and Margaret R. Miles, eds., *Immaculate and Powerful: The Female in Sacred Image and Social Reality* (Boston: Beacon, 1985) 32.

[7] Phyllis Trible, *Texts of Terror* (Philadelphia: Fortress, 1984) 102.

[8] Ibid. 104.

[9] Ibid. 105.

rhetorical analysis is presented in a sympathetic style, intended to encourage compassion for the daughter and other daughters who are trapped in similar circumstances. While her analysis may elicit deep empathy from the reader, it provides no strategy for change. She leaves it to other feminist writers to examine narratives of women victims in the Bible and advocate for change in social structures outside institutional religion.

Esther Fuchs challenges Trible's valorization of the daughter as a victim.[10] The tradition that her sacrifice is the occasion of a yearly lamentation does not do justice to what she suffered. To praise the daughter as a courageous victim is merely to affirm and legitimize the patriarchal nature of the text. Unfortunately, the daughter is portrayed as expendable. Unlike Isaac, whose survival is necessary to maintain the covenant, she is not connected to any major biblical themes. As a daughter living in her father's house she is unattached to another man who might seek revenge for her death. Her disappearance from the narrative and from the history of Israel is, sadly, of no account.

Undoubtedly Jephthah's daughter is a victim of her father's power to decide whether she will live or die. If she is viewed as a hero one has to spiritualize her devotion to her father and/or to God. She thus becomes a martyr for a cause beyond her physical circumstances. As a human being caught in an untenable situation, her most heroic act is her request to leave her father's house and spend time with her women friends.

Each of the writers quoted in this section approaches the text from a feminist perspective, yet each frames her argument differently. The key concern is what constitutes a victim and whether victim status can be used to support feminist societal goals.

## Is Jephthah a Hero or a Victim?

Traditionally, Jephthah has been the focus of this narrative. After all, he was a successful military leader and judge. Other biblical references to Jephthah emphasize that he rescued Israel from its enemies (1 Sam 12:11) and that it was by faith that he "conquered kingdoms, administered justice, obtained promises . . . became mighty in war and put foreign armies to flight" (Heb 11:32-33). With the emphasis on such a resounding record of achievement, the story truly is about Jephthah the judge, who coincidentally has an unfortunate episode involving his daughter.

[10] Esther Fuchs, *Sexual Politics of the Biblical Narrative: Reading the Hebrew Bible as a Woman* (Sheffield: Sheffield Academic Press, 2000) 178.

In spite of the adulation these texts give Jephthah, a case can be made that Jephthah is a victim. Esther Fuchs claims that the narrative portrays him as such, albeit a victim through his own wrongheaded actions.[11] The victim status of his daughter is obvious, but Jephthah suffers as well. The narrative stresses that she is his only daughter—in fact, his only child— and it emphasizes his loss rather than the daughter's ultimate sacrifice. Upon seeing her emerge from the house he sees her innocent joy in contrast to his own grief. Fuchs maintains that, since the daughter comes out of the house of her own free will, some of the blame for her fate rests upon her. Jephthah's words, that she has brought him very low, contrast with the preceding military victory that won him praise. The war hero becomes a victim of his daughter's actions. Thus Jephthah is to be pitied.

Not only does the narrative reinforce hierarchy, placing the father above the daughter, but both father and daughter acknowledge a higher allegiance to God. Jephthah says that he has opened his mouth to the LORD and cannot take back his vow. The daughter says, "My father, if you have opened your mouth to the LORD, do to me according to what has gone out of your mouth." Both father and daughter interpret allegiance to God very narrowly. Neither imagines that there can be a flexible interpretation of God's law. As a result, both can be viewed as victims of their own ignorance and shortsightedness.

Fuchs speculates that if the daughter challenged her father she would actually be challenging God.[12] Her silence and obedience to her father keep the focus on his grief. If she challenged him overtly she, rather than her father, would be the object of sympathy. Likewise, if she challenged Jephthah's vow she would be challenging God. The text simply could not allow such challenges to take place. It is the role of later interpreters, less wedded to a static image of God and a hierarchical theology, to envision other possibilities.

### Why Blame the Victim?

One of the guiding principles for aiding abused women is not to blame the victim for her abusive situation. Modern psychology views abuse as cyclical with the abuser and victim contributing to an escalating pattern of behavior that results in violence. Counselors realize that if there

---

[11] Esther Fuchs, "Marginalization, Ambiguity, Silencing: The Story of Jephthah's Daughter," *Journal of Feminist Studies in Religion* 5 (Spring 1989) 41.
[12] Ibid. 42.

is to be successful intervention the victim must not be condemned for her role in the cycle of violence.

Jephthah's reply to his daughter's greeting blames her for what inevitably must follow. "Alas, my daughter, you have brought me very low [or brought me to my knees]; you have become the cause of great trouble to me" (Judg 11:35). Mieke Bal suggests that another interpretation is possible here. What Jephthah sees at this moment is the loss of his identity.[13] He views his daughter as his only means of perpetuating his line. Consequently, his line will die out with her death.

The narrative of Tamar and Judah in Gen 38:1-30 gives credence to this reading. Judah, son of Jacob, arranges a marriage between his son Er and Tamar. Er dies before inseminating Tamar and then, by the law of levirate marriage, Tamar marries the second son, Onan. Onan is struck dead as well.[14] Frustrated with waiting for Judah to give her his third son, she veils herself and sits at the entrance to Enaim. Judah, thinking she is a harlot, has sex with her. She becomes pregnant and bears twin sons, thus insuring Judah's line and her own security.

Reading Tamar's story intertextually with Judges 11, Bal speculates that Jephthah seems to think that his only chance for perpetuating his line is for him to impregnate his daughter. As Tamar insures her position in Judah's line by having sex with her father-in-law, so perhaps Jephthah contemplates a similar alternative. Thus his anguish at seeing his daughter emerge from his house and his reiteration that she is his only daughter and that she will die point to his desperation. While Jephthah's words blame the victim, the emotion behind them and Jephthah's failure to imagine alternatives for perpetuating his line contribute to the escalation of violence that leads to death.

### Why the Emphasis on Virginity?

The phrase "bewail my virginity" occurs twice in the narrative. The first occurrence is in the daughter's request to go to the mountains to bewail her virginity with her companions. The second use of the phrase follows immediately to describe what they did on the mountains. The narrative states that upon their return, Jephthah's daughter never slept with a man.

The issue here is whether "virginity" in Judges 11 means never having had sex or refers to the daughter's status as a young, pubescent woman. Peggy Day suggests that *betulah*, translated "virginity" *(NRSV)*, designates

---

[13] Bal, *Death & Dissymmetry,* 63.

[14] For the rules regarding levirate marriage see Deut 25:5-10.

a young woman who has reached puberty and is now of marriageable age.[15] In support of this position Day cites the example of Rebekah, who "was very fair to look upon, a *betulah,* whom no man had known" (Gen 24:16). If *betulah* means virgin in the sense of never having had sex it would be redundant to add "whom no man had ever known." Another example occurs in a reference to the four hundred *betulot* from Jabesh-gilead who were turned over to the tribe of Benjamin to repopulate the tribe after a civil war. "And they found four hundred young *betulah* who had never slept with a man and brought them to the camp at Shiloh (Judg 21:12). In Joel 1:8 Israel is called to "lament like a *betulah* dressed in sackcloth for the husband of her youth." In this text it is clear that *betulah* refers to a married woman, one who undoubtedly has had sex. These examples serve to support the idea that the modern concept of "virginity" is not the issue in these texts. It was, however, expected in ancient Israel that a *betulah* would not have had sex prior to marriage. Day further argues that the young women go to the mountains to take part in a ritual marking the death of one stage of life (girlhood) and entry into another (marriage).

Mieke Bal discusses two more texts that support the notion that virginity means nubility or marriageability, not a technical physical condition. In two horrifying narratives women are offered as sexual objects to placate angry mobs. In one instance a man of Gibeah is hosting a Levite and the Levite's wife (perhaps secondary wife or concubine) in his home when an angry mob surrounds the house demanding that the Levite be released so that the mob can have sex with him. The host berates the mob and then makes an offer. "Here are my *betulah* daughter and [the Levite's] concubine; let me bring them out now. Ravish them and do whatever you want to them; but against this man do not do such a vile thing" (Judg 19:24). The mob seizes the wife and rapes her through the night. Nothing is said about what happens to the daughter, which indicates she is not important to the story. Bal claims that if virginity was more desirable to the men they would have seized the daughter. The daughter is available and apparently unused. Instead, the men abuse the Levite's wife.[16]

The incident at Gibeah is an echo of a Genesis narrative in which the men of Sodom demand that Lot send out his two male visitors so that the mob might have sex with them. Lot intercedes on behalf of his guests. As a solution Lot pleads, "Look, I have two daughters who have not known a man; let me bring them out to you, and do to them as you please; only do

[15] Peggy Day, "From the Child Is Born the Woman: The Story of Jephthah's Daughter," in eadem, *Gender and Difference in Ancient Israel* (Minneapolis: Fortress, 1989) 59.
[16] Bal, *Death & Dissymmetry,* 47.

nothing to these men" (Gen 19:8). The word *betulah* is not used here, but the implication is that his daughters are sexually mature women who are made available for rape.

It should be noted that others do read *betulah* to reflect physical virginity. If this is so, the phrase "never knew a man" is in apposition to *betulah*. If this reading is correct, then the time on the mountains would be a time of mourning the daughter's childless state rather than a rite-of-passage ritual. This option will be discussed below.

## *Where Is the Mother?*

According to the biblical account, Jephthah's daughter appears to have no mother. This may be explained by Jephthah's own upbringing. His mother is said to have been a harlot. Perhaps Jephthah's daughter was born of a harlot as well. Bal speculates further that Jephthah's upbringing as a son of a harlot influenced his later life. In her analysis Bal claims that when the brothers of the proper wife expelled Jephthah, this motivated him to prove himself as a warrior. Jephthah may have felt he had license to kill his daughter.[17] Bal suggests that Jephthah's displacement from his father's home is a form of domestic violence that later finds its way into the political arena of war.[18] The daughter eventually pays with her life for the conflicts society is unable to resolve.

The experiences of other mothers mentioned in Judges can be read intertexually to suggest possible roles for the daughter's mother. Perhaps she was a harlot like Jephthah's mother and did not participate in raising her daughter. Perhaps she was as powerless to act as Sisera's mother, who peered out of the window waiting for her son to return from battle (Judg 5:28). We can imagine the daughter's mother awaiting the return of her daughter from her two months in the mountains. The mother's friends might try to allay her anxiety with optimistic excuses and wishes. Like Sisera's mother, she is powerless to affect her child's fate. Or maybe she is receptive to the ways of God and tries to communicate her wisdom to her husband, as did Samson's mother (Judg 13:1-25). Perhaps, like Samson's mother, she is not privy to what is about to happen to her child.[19] We have no information about this particular mother, although her absence certainly seeks an explanation.

---

[17] Ibid. 199.

[18] Ibid. 231.

[19] Samson chooses not to confide in his parents but conceals his plot to trick the Philistines (Judg 14:5-20).

## What Did the Women Do on the Mountain?

As mentioned above, there are at least two possible explanations of how the women companions spent their time on the mountain.[20] If they were engaged in a rite-of-passage ceremony they probably would be marking the transition from girlhood to womanhood that occurs at first menstruation. Mieke Bal describes three stages in this transition. Each is marked by a different Hebrew word for a young woman. A *na'arah* is a young girl who is still under the protection of her father. A *betulah* is a pubescent young woman who is physically able to conceive. An *'almah* is a woman who is married or pledged to a man but not yet pregnant. A *betulah* is in a stage of insecurity and danger because she is between the protection of two men, her father and her husband.[21] These nubile women will not be secure until they are married and produce offspring in their husband's family. Thus the companions' time on the mountain is a time of insecurity.

According to Arnold van Gennep a rite of passage includes three phases: a preliminal phase of separation, a liminal phase of transition, and a postliminal phase of incorporation.[22] If we apply van Gennep's phases to Judges 11, the rite of separation would occur when the daughter requests time to go to the mountains. She specifies the location, duration, and who she wants to accompany her. The liminal phase of transition invites speculation as to what the young women actually did. For Jephthah's daughter the postliminal phase will not end in a transition to a new family, but in her death.

The Tanakh offers evidence for the separation of women during menstruation (Lev 15:19-33).[23] A menstruating woman was considered ritually unclean for the seven days of her period. During that time anyone who touched her or the objects on which she sat or slept was also considered unclean and subject to purification.[24] A natural outgrowth of this practice might be to segregate young menstruating women for a period of time. We

[20] The *NRSV* translation "companions" comes from the Hebrew root *r'h*, which occurs in the feminine plural, indicating that only women comprised the group.

[21] Bal, *Death & Dissymmetry*, 48.

[22] Arnold van Gennep, *The Rites of Passage* (Chicago: University of Chicago Press, 1960) 11. For references to rite of passage research after van Gennep see Day, "From a Child is Born a Woman," 68 n. 7.

[23] Leviticus contains collections of purity laws edited either during or after the Babylonian exile. We are assuming a post-exilic date for the completion of Judges. Thus the concept of separation based on purity regulations could support a coming-of-age ceremony for women upon first menstruation.

[24] Ritual impurity meant that the person deemed unclean could not approach the tabernacle or holy things during the time of uncleanness.

can imagine that the liminal stage would consist of a purification ceremony containing ceremonial bathing, washing garments, and/or animal sacrifice. Based on Leviticus 15, the postliminal phase or incorporation might include an appearance before a religious official before being declared ritually clean. (Cross-cultural anthropological studies of rites of passage for young women could lend support to this practice.)

Since the text states that the women mourned the daughter's lifelong virginity and that she would never know fulfillment as a wife and mother, we can imagine that the time on the mountain might be fraught with fear. The women's own fears could be reflected in the daughter's plight. What kind of man was Jephthah? What kind of man would they marry? Would they be accepted into their husband's family? Would they produce sons? If not, what then? In a culture that placed such a high priority on women bearing sons these were important issues.

The second possibility is that the women engaged in a mourning ceremony on the mountain. There is ample evidence that women mourned the dead. Perhaps the women participated in a ceremony to prepare the daughter for her death. We have no evidence of such a practice. We are left wondering that these women did during their stay on the mountain.

## Why Did She Return to Her Father?

The narrative never mentions the possibility that Jephthah's daughter would not return to her father. In Judges 19 another woman flees from her home. This woman leaves her husband, who plausibly brutalized her judging by his subsequent actions. She returns to her father's home. Her husband hunts her down and forces her to return with him.

If the daughter had not returned after two months, would Jephthah, like the Levite, have searched for her to bring her back? Why does she return of her own volition? What does this behavior suggest in a scenario of abuse? In Alicia Ostriker's performance piece, "Jephthah's Daughter: A Lament," she offers a rationale. "If a baby is beaten by a parent, and then put down on the floor, the baby will crawl, not away from the parent, but toward. So we. So we."[25] Ostriker reads this narrative against the backdrop of domestic violence. Modern psychology speaks of a cycle of violence in which tension builds until the more powerful party abuses the victim. The abuser then apologizes and is forgiven by the victim. After a cooling-off

---

[25] Alicia Ostriker, "Jephthah's Daughter: A Lament," in Jane Schaberg, Alice Bach, and Esther Fuchs, eds., *On The Cutting Edge: The Study of Women in Biblical Worlds* (New York: Continuum, 2003) 240. See appendix for the entire poem.

period, the cycle repeats. The cycle is kept in motion by the victim's love for the partner, hope that things will change, and fear of more violence. Ostriker's example of an abused baby turning back to its parent exemplifies the love and hope phases of the cycle.[26] If this cycle is operative in the Jephthah narrative, then the daughter returns out of love and loyalty, perhaps hoping that her father will change his mind.

## What Was the Nature of the Annual Ceremony?

The Judges 11 narrative ends with a brief reference to a custom that was said to have arisen after the daughter's death, in which the daughters of Israel lamented the daughter of Jephthah for four days every year. The ceremony is not mentioned again and has not come down to modern times. We do not know its precise content. Unlike other annual rituals described in the Tanakh, it does not commemorate God's involvement in Israel's history, but rather remembers a human being who is not linked with a significant historical event. In addition, the ceremony is distinctive in that it is founded by women in memory of a woman.

The Tanakh refers to women performing ritual acts, either in addition to the Israelite cult or outside the cult. The Deuteronomistic editor condemns these actions. For example, Jezebel and Athaliah are associated with the cult of the goddess Asherah. Other women make offerings to the Queen of Heaven, kneading dough, making cakes, pouring out libations, and burning incense to her (Jer 7:16-20; 44:15-19, 25). In Ezek 8:14 women, seated at the gate of the Temple of the LORD, weep for the Babylonian fertility god Tammuz. These women perform a ritual lamentation for a foreign god in the Temple precincts. Susan Ackerman suggests that because women had so little opportunity to participate in the official Israelite cult they found these opportunities outside the cult.[27]

Women performed ritual mourning for the dead in Israel. These actions included wearing sackcloth, tearing clothes, baring part of the body, beating the breast, and wailing. In other examples of mourning rituals, the daughters of Israel are called to weep over Saul (2 Sam 1:24). The daughters of Rabbah are to cry, gird themselves with sackcloth, and run to and fro among the hedges (Jer 49:3). Laments uttered by Jeremiah on the occasion of Josiah's death are passed down by the singing men and women (2 Chr

[26] Alicia Ostriker, "Jephthah's Daughter," *Cross Currents* 51 (Summer 2001), available on-line at EBSCOhost.

[27] Susan Ackerman, *Warrior, Dancer, Seductress, Queen: Women in Judges and Biblical Israel* (New York: Doubleday, 1998) 116.

35:25). Rizpah, daughter of Aiah, spreads sackcloth on the ground as a bed and holds a vigil over the desecrated bodies of Saul and Jonathan (2 Sam 21:10-14).

In addition to the mourning of individuals, women were called to mourn national crises. They raised emotional fervor over impending doom and passed that skill on to subsequent generations. Skilled women were called to mourn the tragedy about to befall Judah in 587 B.C.E.: "Let them quickly raise a dirge over us, so that their eyes may run down with tears and our eyelids flow with water" (Jer 9:18). These women were also told to teach their daughters a dirge and their neighbor a lament (Jer 9:20).

The custom of women mourners appears throughout the Mediterranean world over the millennia and continues today. In the Gospel of Luke women beat their breasts and wail, anticipating apocalyptic calamity (Luke 23:27-28). Though there are few instances reported in written history, the tradition of women sharing their grief does, in fact, survive.

Drawing upon references in the Bible to occasions of women's mourning, we can suggest possible components for the annual ceremony. Perhaps women skilled in mourning gathered the other women on a mountaintop to keen laments, such as the one credited to David in 2 Sam 1:19-27, which contain personal elements relating specifically to the deceased. It is likely that in this case the lament would include a retelling of Jephthah's daughter's tragedy. The women might have offered sacrifices of grain or libations, which suggest an alternative to the tragedy of human sacrifice. The women would have needed food for their four-day vigil. Perhaps they baked special cakes, like the ones baked for the Queen of Heaven in Jer 7:18. Like the daughters of Rabbah, the women might have engaged in ecstatic wailing and dancing. It appears that regardless of the content of the ritual, it was done outside the official Israelite cult. This could account for its being mentioned only once in the Bible.

Their ritual undoubtedly encompassed the experiences of grief contemporary to women's experience. Ethnographic studies of mourning in the Middle East support the idea that women went to cemeteries daily to lament the dead and unburden their own hearts.[28] A heightened emotional ritual might provide a liminal catharsis in which the women shared their pain and prepared to return to their everyday lives.

Another possibility for the annual ceremony commemorating Jephthah's daughter's death is that it was a woman's life-cycle ritual in which the story of Jephthah's daughter served as an etiology for the rite. Peggy Day

---

[28] Barbara Miller, "Women, Death, and Mourning in the Ancient Eastern Mediterranean World" (Ph.D. diss., University of Michigan-Ann Arbor, 1994) 294.

suggests that the Greek myths of Iphigenia and Kore/Persephone parallel the narrative of Jephthah's daughter and offer possibilities for the nature of the annual ceremony.[29]

Day cites traditions of Iphigenia in Euripides' two plays, *Iphigenia in Aulis* and *Iphigenia in Tauris* (fifth century B.C.E.). In these plays Agamemnon vows to sacrifice to the goddess Artemis the loveliest thing born that year, which, of course, is his daughter Iphigenia. Iphigenia is brought to Aulis under the pretext of becoming Achilles' bride. In the end Iphigenia is not sacrificed; an animal is substituted for her. She spends her life serving in the sanctuary of Artemis. Evidence from an Artemis sanctuary near Athens shows that young girls participated in a ritual of seclusion before marriage. Although the ritual requires that a girl be sacrificed, an animal may be substituted for her. Young girls were required to participate in this ceremony before marriage, suggesting that this rite-of-passage ritual was linked to a legend similar to the narrative of Jephthah's daughter.[30] Perhaps the ceremony in Judges 11 denoted the seclusion of young women prior to marriage when they offered sacrifices before assuming the role of wife and mother.

Another Greek legend with parallels to the story of Jephthah's daughter and a ceremony marking a transition to womanhood is the Kore/Persephone myth. The maiden Kore is abducted by Hades into the underworld and is rescued by the god Hermes, who returns her to her mother Demeter. The girl who descends to the underworld returns as a fertile woman. This transition from one state to another is accompanied by a name change (Kore becomes Persephone), recognizing her new status. An annual women's festival, Thesmophoria, celebrates this myth. In the three-day ceremony women recall Kore's descent to the underworld as they process up a hill, retell the myth, fast, and make lamentation. On the third day a banquet is held. Originally the Kore myth might have been connected to female puberty rites and/or fertility rites within marriage.

An obvious difference between the Kore/Persephone legend and Jephthah's daughter is that Kore is immortal and the daughter is mortal. As a goddess, Kore will be reborn in another form, while Jephthah's daughter dies. Jephthah's daughter will never experience rebirth into womanhood. Day sees Iphigenia, Kore, and Jephthah's daughter as adolescent girls on the brink of womanhood. While Iphigenia and Kore successfully negotiate the transition, Jephthah's daughter does not. Day suggests that Jephthah's

---

[29] Day, "From the Child Is Born the Woman," 60.

[30] Thomas C. Römer argues that the author of Judges 11 knew the legends of Iphigenia and modeled his text after them. See Thomas C. Römer, "Why Would the Deuteronomists Tell About the Sacrifice of Jephthah's Daughter?" *JSOT* 77 (1998) 27–38.

daughter's quick consent to her father's dilemma is a mark of immaturity in that she does not consider her own well-being. A successful transition to womanhood involves responsible actions on one's own behalf.

## Where Is God?

As noted in the discussion of the rabbis in Chapter Four, God seems to withdraw from the narrative. God, who intervened to save Isaac, no longer intervenes to save individuals. In Judges, God guides national interests as opposed to individual interests. Frymer-Kensky claims that the world of Judges is like the world of today, where some do not expect God to intervene directly. Instead, human beings and the social systems they develop are designed to prevent such tragedies.[31] At the time portrayed in Judges, social systems allowed male householders broad discretion. A husband or father was within his rights to do whatever he wanted within the household. He was responsible to God but, without any social institutions to interpret that duty, cruel personal choices sometimes prevailed. Frymer-Kensky claims that Judges 11 is pivotal in that the narrative indicates that uncontrolled patriarchy will subsequently lead to the destruction of the social order. Clearly this is born out in the rest of the book of Judges. The fate of the Levite's wife is final proof. The question remains: where is God? The biblical story presents a partial answer in the establishment of the monarchy, Temple, and prophets. For all the flaws inherent in this new social system, a more unified acknowledgment of God's role and rule provides hope for the future.

Exum discusses the silence of God in this narrative. In her view Jephthah was not faithless in making his vow.[32] His vow was a sign of his piety and confidence in God. The text is not critical of either the making or the execution of the vow. The death of the daughter is not punishment for Jephthah's vow. There is no indication that God rejects Jephthah as God rejected Saul. The only direct act God performs is to deliver the Ammonites into the hands of the Israelites. God's silent transcendence raises questions about the goodness of God. Exum claims that Jephthah faces a world in which unrelated events conspire to overwhelm, where a victorious warrior returning from battle can meet tragedy at the threshold of his house. Where is God? God's presence is elusive. It appears that God is present in national crises, but not as accessible in personal crises.

---

[31] Frymer-Kensky, *Reading the Women of the Bible,* 116.
[32] J. Cheryl Exum, *Tragedy and Biblical Narrative* (Cambridge: Cambridge University Press, 1992) 58.

## What Does This Narrative Say about Violence?

The reader of Judges 11 can be quick to judge Jephthah and blame him solely for the brutal death of his daughter. Exum cautions against such a simplistic reading. The cycle of violence is too complicated to permit blaming one person or one event for tragic events that follow.[33] Jephthah made a vow in a crisis situation. It makes little difference whether he made it because of faith or lack of faith in God. The vow was made. The cycle of violence becomes more complex when, unbeknownst to Jephthah, his daughter emerges from his house. When the daughter complies with her father's vow she joins the patriarchal forces that lead to her death. If she had resisted overtly she might have been able to interrupt the unfortunate series of events. Exum sees that the women who commemorate her as a victim reinforce the inevitability of the cycle of violence. It would appear that violence is partially beyond human control.

While the cycle of violence seems inevitable, hope is present. Although the daughter complies with her father's vow, she offers some resistance. Her words shift the blame for her fate back onto her father: "*[Y]ou* have opened *your* mouth to the LORD; do to me according to what has gone forth from *your* mouth."[34]

When the daughter requests time away with her friends she interrupts the immediacy of her death. The time of respite opens the narrative to the possibility that a way will be found to avert her death. The shift from the patriarchal world to the world of women offers hope that women's solidarity can overcome tragedy. As the women segregate themselves, they are free to imagine strategies for the future. Gerda Lerner claims that in such a circumstance women can come to a new understanding of their social reality. This feminist consciousness emerges in four stages.[35] First there is an awareness of a wrong. Second is a development of a sense of sisterhood. Third, new strategies are developed. Fourth, a new vision for the future emerges. The first steps in a strategy for change are present in the story. The reader is left to imagine new strategies and partake in a new vision of women in society. The challenge begins in the biblical period and stretches ever onward.

[33] J. Cheryl Exum, "On Judges 11," in Athalya Brenner, ed., *A Feminist Companion to Judges* (Sheffield: Sheffield Academic Press, 1993) 140.

[34] Exum, *Fragmented Women,* 40.

[35] Gerda Lerner, *The Creation of Patriarchy* (New York: Oxford University Press, 1986) 242.

## Summary

The narrative of Jephthah's daughter has been of particular interest to feminist interpreters. The mistreatment of a daughter by her father resonates with abusive behavior in our own time. The varied interpretations attempt primarily to understand the pitfalls of patriarchal systems of domination. In so doing they expose values such as justice, loyalty, and responsibility that transcend time and social location. In the next chapter the feminists will engage in a conversation with the ancient rabbis about values.

# CHAPTER SIX

## *The Rabbis and the Feminists Converse About Values*

At the beginning of this project it seemed to me that the medieval rabbis would have little in common with modern feminist interpreters. The rabbis, who upheld the patriarchal order of their day, and the feminists, who eschew patriarchal social and religious systems, seem unlikely conversation partners. In this chapter we will examine the values each group brings to its analysis of Judges 11. While each group is bound by its own time period, history, and social setting, each also professes values that transcend time and place. These values will be the basis of this rabbi-feminist conversation.

Values can be defined as principles or standards that have ultimate significance for a group or an individual. In a religious sense values are principles that reflect and enact the attributes of God. One way that Judeo-Christian traditions convey these values is by using anthropomorphic images of God. In these images God speaks and acts on behalf of what are claimed to be God's own values. For example, when the angel of the LORD orders Abraham to refrain from executing Isaac, the writer of the text (as well as the believing community behind the text) portrays God as one who affirms human life rather than human sacrifice. In the angel's second pronouncement the value of human life is further specified and expanded in the covenant promise that Abraham's offspring will be a blessing for the whole world (Gen 22:15-17). In this instance Abraham's obedience elicits the blessing. This text is meant to illustrate that God values life, blessing, and obedience.

We have noted that the Deuteronomistic editing of Judges depicts a cyclical pattern of God punishing disobedience by allowing enemies to capture tribal territories and then raising up effective leaders as a reward

94

for obedience. In addition, God's presence diminishes during the course of the book. The book ends with no reference to God; instead "everyone did what was right in their own eyes" (Judg 21:25). In Judg 11:29-40 the Spirit of the LORD ensures Jephthah's military success, but God is absent as the consequences of Jephthah's vow are played out. God's apparent absence complicates our attempts to determine the values that underlie the narrative. Jephthah is obedient to what he understands to be his commitment to his vow. However, life and blessing do not prevail; death and national chaos result. Within these murky shadows of confusion the rabbis and the feminists engage in dialogue about values and the nature of God.

## Rabbinic Values

The post-biblical writings of Mishnah, Talmud, and Midrash comprise an effort by the rabbis to understand and appreciate multi-leveled interpretations of the Bible. The Torah was seen as the basis for living. The ethical teaching and moral precepts behind its laws and narratives required constant reinterpretation in light of historical and social change. The comments of the rabbis reflect their basic social assumptions and the questions they bring to the text, as well as the values they want to convey. The multiplicity of voices in rabbinic literature is testimony to a variety of opinions about the application of biblical values to everyday life.

According to Max Kadushin, the rabbis begin with a set of core values that are intrinsic to their work, including justice, love, Torah, and Israel. These values are interwoven and are said to form the basis of Jewish life. They grow out of a shared understanding of God, the world, and human life.[1] In the midrash on Judges 11 the rabbis are concerned with justice, family loyalty (love), compassion, tradition (Torah), and allegiance to Israel. Besides controlling interpersonal relationships, these values also shape an understanding of the relationship between God and the individual.

### Justice

The concept of justice in Jewish life grows out of an ethical framework based on human relationships and responsibilities within community life and relationship to God. Justice is not abstract in Judaism. It is articulated as laws (teachings) and behavior. Practitioners of justice were

---

[1] Max Kadushin is quoted in the introduction to Reuven Hammer, *The Classic Midrash* (New York: Paulist, 1995) 30.

expected to know the laws, exercise wisdom in making judgments, and make themselves available for consultation. The midrash on Judges 11 upholds the laws of justice but is critical of the practitioners. The rule against human sacrifice is clear. It is assumed the practitioners would know that the daughter could have been redeemed with an animal sacrifice. In *Targum Jonathan of the Former Prophets* Jephthah is blamed for not consulting Phinehas, the priest. His uninformed action resulted in a ruling that a man was not to offer his son or daughter as a holocaust (Tg. Jon. 11:39). In *Genesis Rabbah* both Jephthah and the high priest are blamed for being too arrogant to seek justice. Both men shirked their duty as leaders and failed to uphold the established process of justice. The rabbis reflect a debate within their own circles regarding making and fulfilling vows. They agree that the daughter's death was not required. They disagree as to whether an animal sacrifice could be a substitute or whether the vow was invalid from the start. Both positions affirm justice for the innocent victim, contrary to the biblical outcome.

The rabbis find justice for Jephthah and Phinehas by imagining physical punishment (gradual loss of limbs) or spiritual punishment (withdrawal of God's spirit). Both these forms of punishment seem to require otherworldly intervention. Their radical nature might indicate limitations for exacting punishment within the medieval Jewish legal system. The rabbis may have chosen to comment on the Jephthah narrative because it illustrated their call for judicial reform.

Another criticism of the judicial system might be behind the suggestion that the daughter sought justice from the wise men (elders) in Pseudo-Philo. Seila and her companions tell their plight to the wise men, but no one responds to them. An explanation follows in which God is said to close the mouths of the sages. Can this imply that the judicial system is ineffectual or that its decisions are contrary to those of God? God claims to have a plan that is not to be foiled. God congratulates Seila for her wisdom that exceeds the wisdom of her father and the elders and then claims that her death will be precious in God's sight. It would appear that God champions a strict interpretation of the keeping of a vow. This incident seems to reflect a more rigid rabbinic position on vows. In either case the justice system fails, the innocent daughter suffers, and justice remains elusive.

## Family Loyalty (Love)

The midrashim on this narrative portray Jephthah's daughter as loyal to her father and by extension loyal to God. Upon her father's return from battle she learns about his vow and immediately acknowledges her role as a daughter subject to her father's will. Almost as an afterthought she requests a time of respite, followed by her return to her father. While some rabbis imagine that she goes to the elders for help, they all portray her as returning rather than trying to escape her fate.

Pseudo-Philo describes the daughter's deep desire to marry and thus maintain the role society expects of her. In her impassioned lament she appeals to her mother, who has been preparing for her daughter's wedding, and pleads with the entire cosmos to hear her case. One by one she enumerates the wedding details her mother has undertaken. Not only will her mother's blend of anointing oils and the newly woven garment go unused, they will be consumed by the earth and be no more. Seila speaks of her deepest grief to her mother, "In vain have you borne your only daughter." Seila is loyal to her father but intimately connected with her mother.

## Compassion

The value of compassion is expressed in the conversation between the daughter and her father. If we view compassion as a willingness to share the suffering of another, then the daughter appears more compassionate than her father. In Pseudo-Philo, Jephthah grows faint when he sees his daughter come from his house. He blames her and asks, "Who will put my heart in the balance and my soul in the scale?" His demeanor is tragic. He is deeply moved and conflicted over what will take place. However, his concern is more for himself than for his daughter. When he allows her to go to the mountains, the only verbal response he can manage is "Go."

The daughter, however, shows compassion for her father. Her response overcompensates for her father's self-indulgence. It appears that the magnitude of the impending tragedy produces what could be interpreted as exaggerated compassion. With no one intervening in the situation, emotions reign.

Compassion is evident in the behavior of the women who accompany the daughter to the mountains so that she can weep and tell her story. In Pseudo-Philo the women bury the daughter, weep for her, establish the annual commemoration, and name her tomb "Seila." The rabbis enhance the theme of compassion by elaborating the role that the women play.

## Respect for Torah Traditions

The rabbis condemn Jephthah for carrying out human sacrifice. They cite Lev 18:21, "You shall not give any of your offspring to sacrifice them to Molech, and so profane the name of your God." Offering human sacrifice is punishable by stoning (Lev 20:2-5). They recall Jeremiah's condemnation of the nation for sacrificing their children in the valley of Hinnom (Jer 7:31). The full weight of Jeremiah's criticism against Judah is brought to bear against Jephthah (*b. Ta'anit* 4a). The gravity of the ramifications of Jephthah's vow strikes at the heart of Israelite teachings.

Yet another Torah text provides clarification about the offering of sacrifices. The writer of *Tanhuma B* cites Leviticus 1, specifying that animals are appropriate sacrifices, and Lev 21:1, citing the redemption price for a human being. This midrash clearly states that God did not require that Abraham sacrifice Isaac. The rabbis are concerned that laws in Torah must be maintained. Perhaps the entire Jephthah episode is a result of his ignorance of the traditions. Thus the narrative serves as a warning to those ignorant of the law.

The rabbis recall Abraham (Eliezer), Caleb, and Saul in an attempt to condemn Jephthah's act, but they subvert the intention of these original stories to fit their own agendas. None of these biblical stories deals with asking God for a favor. The writers of the midrash insert this issue in response either to the Jephthah narrative itself or to a specific circumstance in their day. Since the making and keeping of vows is so heavily emphasized in the Mishnah and Talmud, the midrash on Jephthah could have originated in this milieu. The rabbis were free to manipulate the texts as they chose.

## Allegiance to Israel

The biblical writers and rabbis are concerned with the preservation of the people of Israel. At various points in history "Israel" has been defined as a political state, but more broadly Israel refers to a people. The time frame of the Jephthah story is pre-monarchical Israel, when the Israelites set a priority on acquiring and securing land held by foreigners. Jephthah's victory over the Ammonites briefly secured land and peace but eventually resulted in civil war with the tribe of Ephraim. The historian Josephus praises Jephthah's victory: "[He] freed his own people from that slavery which they had undergone for eighteen years." Josephus then proceeds to deprecate Jephthah's military victory in light of the sacrifice of the daughter a "calamity no way correspondent to the great actions he had done."

The daughter champions a claim to the land as well. In Pseudo-Philo, Seila is willing to put her life on the line with the words, "And who is there who would be sad in death, seeing the people freed?" She is obsessed with whether she will be a proper (unblemished) sacrifice. This is the concern she takes to the mountains. Her loyalty and allegiance inspire her fervor to carry out the sacrifice.

## God and Humans

The rabbis seek to maintain the sovereignty of God in the face of human disaster. In *Tanhuma B* the Holy Spirit cries out to Jephthah, "Did I want you to sacrifice human lives to me? I commanded not Abraham to slay his son, but rather 'Lay not thine hand upon the lad.'" God's will is revealed through the Torah, and ignorance of the Torah does not justify Jephthah's action. God works no miracle to save the daughter; rather, humans are the agents of Torah teachings, even when the example they set is a negative one.

In Pseudo-Philo, Seila seeks advice from the sages, who are unable to respond to her. God claims responsibility for closing the mouths of these wise men. It appears that the deity orchestrates events to insure her death and then compliments the daughter for having wisdom. If God manipulates justice merely to teach Jephthah a lesson, then God is neither just nor compassionate, but one who plays games with human lives. Some would want to abandon God at this point. Others might speculate that God is limited by a preponderance of careless human acts. This image limits God to the machinations of human behavior. Perhaps a more satisfying image drawn from these rabbinic texts sees God as one who reveals a way of life to humans through the teachings of the Torah. In this respect Torah and the accompanying discourse on it are one. The rabbis maintained the concept that both the written and subsequent oral interpretations were revealed at Sinai. The revelation provides direction, and God's presence is manifest in living out the revelation.

## Can a Proto-Feminist Voice Be Discerned in the Rabbinic Midrash?

A case can be made that a proto-feminist voice is heard in the midrash on Judges 11. While acknowledging that males wrote the midrash and that the portrayal of the daughter is a male creation, we cannot deny that some rabbis place the daughter at the center of their midrash to expose injustices. She is a pivotal character through whom flaws in the social system can be critiqued.

In *Tanhuma B* the daughter defends herself to her father. She speaks of the joy she feels when she greets him. She argues that the Torah prescribes animal sacrifices, not human sacrifices. When Jephthah counters with the importance of keeping a vow she responds, claiming that Jacob and Hannah made vows, but neither involved human sacrifice. She participates in a typical rabbinic exchange, citing Scripture to support her position. The conversation between father and daughter exposes the lack of understanding concerning vows, but it does not critique the patriarchal system itself. Jephthah may be shamed, but he retains his position as judge. He still has life-and-death power over his daughter.

In Pseudo-Philo, God says that the daughter is wiser than the father and more perceptive than the sages. What is this wisdom of a young woman that exceeds that of a ruler and the sages? It appears it is the knowledge that she will die, and her willingness to die is what distinguishes her. In the same midrash the rabbis highlight the world of women in the daughter's lament over her doomed marriage. The voice here is sensitive to a young girl's concern. The details about the women mourning and burying her and then memorializing her illustrate the time-honored responsibilities of women. The tone of the lament and the women's actions are more than just a report of their activities. The emotion of the lament and reference to a women's ceremony, although it has since disappeared from tradition, suggest that this is the most woman-centered midrash in this collection. While this material is not overtly feminist, it might be labeled "proto-feminist." It opens a door for feminists of later generations to explore women's role in patriarchal society and to fashion their own midrash.

## Feminist Values

In our feminist interpretation of the Bible we have placed an otherwise marginalized character, specifically a woman, at the center of our analysis of androcentric texts. We have noted how Jephthah's daughter is a victim of social injustice and that, for the most part, she accepts that role. This conflicts with an important aspect of feminism—namely, actively developing strategies that work for equality between women and men. We will now discuss a feminist approach to the daughter's story as it relates to the values of justice, loyalty, compassion, responsibility, respect, and a commitment to liberation.

### Justice

A major difference between a rabbinic critique of Judges 11 and a feminist critique is that the rabbis are calling for justice (reform) within the confines of the patriarchal social structure of medieval Judaism. Feminists broadly critique the structure of patriarchal society and its religious institutions. Transformation from a patriarchal or hierarchical social system to one of equality is not a matter of tweaking the system; it calls for radical change and reorientation of values.

The fact that the daughter is nameless exposes the patriarchal character of the biblical writers and patriarchal injustice within family life. The text describes Jephthah's daughter in her various roles as a child of her father, as a virgin, and as a victim. The reader's sympathy is aroused, but there is no call for social change. Adele Reinhartz claims that her namelessness and her role as a daughter call attention to the injustices within the family. Challenging the power structure of the basic unit of both ancient and modern society is a radical call for justice. It is easy to make a historical argument that women were more oppressed in ancient societies and that their lot has improved. For the feminists this viewpoint abdicates responsibility and fails to fully implement the change necessary to bring about equality.

## Loyalty: Female Bonding

The first step in a feminist liberation strategy is to recognize that one is oppressed. Such consciousness-raising usually occurs within groups in which the participants articulate their own experience of oppression. The gathering of the women on the mountain invites speculation about what might have happened there. The daughter might have been seen as a role model of obedience to authority or, conversely, as a warning to other women against blind obedience. The daughter becomes an archetypal figure that the other women could recognize in their own experience. If the gathering was part of a puberty rite, the communication among the women might have included strategies for self-recognition and equity in their new households.

Traditionally, women have been denied positions of power in society. Their opportunities to achieve leadership depend on the building of a power base. Feminists propose that creating new myths and constructing new rituals can be a basis for consciousness-raising and empowerment. Sometimes this calls for recognition of an archetypal martyr figure like Jephthah's daughter. These terrifying stories, long ignored, can clarify modern inequities.

Renita Weems speculates that when the women wept in the annual ceremony they did not weep "out of some morbid fascination with the past," but that the weeping helped clarify their vision.[2] The daughter was not the

---

[2] Renita J. Weems, *Just a Sister Away: A Womanist Vision of Women's Relationships in the Bible* (San Diego: LauraMedia, 1988) 66.

first, or the last, to be treated unjustly. The women became "priestesses of sorrow" in that they, with God, lamented the foolishness of human sin. In this way remembrance redeemed the daughter by giving her a place in history. According to Weems, the story is really about women's devotion to each other.

The bonding that took place on the mountain was a sharing of sorrows that can only be shared with other women.[3] As is the case with victims of abuse today, if the shame a woman feels can be shared at all, it is likely to be shared with another woman. Unexpressed feelings of isolation and betrayal easily turn inward, and the victim may come to blame herself. Family loyalty can mask abuse. However, if the focus is shifted from the victim to sharing feeling with others and taking action, change can occur.

## Compassion

Upon Jephthah's return, his daughter identifies with her father's distress to the extent that she willingly abdicates her life in his interest. Her exaggerated form of compassion is so extreme that it blinds her to the injustice done to her, requiring almost total self-denial. The request for time with her friends shows that she might have had second thoughts but, in the end, her sense of compassion and loyalty force her to return. Furthermore, in this narrative, compassion is wrapped in the guise of loyalty to God. Misplaced compassion, like misplaced loyalty, can reinforce oppression. The text invites a critique of the conceptualization of God that simply reinforces hierarchical social structures.

## Responsibility

Both Jephthah and his daughter contribute to the situation that culminates in her death. Jephthah lacks foresight in making the vow, and he later lacks the imagination to save his daughter's life. He blames her for what should be his responsibility. In turn, the reader of the narrative blames him for the tragedy. Merely blaming the victim or the perpetrator of violence leads nowhere.

The daughter also fails to take responsibility for her own fate by not resisting her father. Modern readers speculate that she lacked the self-esteem necessary to speak boldly to her father. If any blame is appropriate to this narrative, it must be placed on hierarchical structures that perpetuate inequalities.

[3] Ibid. 58.

## Respect for Tradition Reassessed

Feminist analysis raises questions concerning the value of biblical texts that depict violence done to women or texts that are misogynistic. It asserts that Jews and Christians who consider these writings as Sacred Scripture must resist the inclination to accommodate to the androcentric authority of the text. Elisabeth Schüssler Fiorenza advocates an approach that raises one's consciousness about the power relations inscribed in the text itself and subsequent interpretations.[4] Such a strategy for reading the Bible aids us in critiquing power structures in our own time. Recognizing that Jephthah had life-and-death power over his daughter raises questions concerning rights of parents today to abuse and control children. In today's Western society numerous laws and the social service agencies administering them reflect the need to protect children.

It is unsettling to question the patriarchal imprint on Scripture and thus confront comfortable beliefs; images of God, institutional structures, and the Bible itself are called into question. The Bible becomes a means of viewing the complexities of the modern world. The human drama of the ancient world is the human drama of today. The Bible may be viewed as a wrestling partner. It is adversarial in its androcentricism, but it also invites a creative impulse to actively affirm liberation and justice. Ongoing dialogue that encompasses a variety of voices can renew the relevance of biblical texts.

Let us imagine the mindset of the author of Judges 11. The author carefully chose how the narrative would unfold, how God would be portrayed, and what role the daughter would play. The story the writer creates is born out of his own time and social circumstance. The modern reader can enter into conversation with the writer by affirming, questioning, or rejecting the writer's agenda, while keeping in mind their differing social locations. According to Weems, a good writer may have anticipated the readers' questions.[5] If this is so, then the author of Judges 11 could expect readers to be horrified, even sickened by the violence in the narrative. The resisting reader understands the writer's intent and is free to imagine strategies for change. This is not to say that biblical writers anticipated feminist questions, but narratives depicting violence against women undoubtedly would shock ancient and modern readers alike.

---

[4] Elisabeth Schüssler Fiorenza, *Wisdom Ways: Introducing Feminist Biblical Interpretation* (Maryknoll, NY: Orbis, 2001) 47.

[5] Renita J. Weems, *Battered Love: Marriage, Sex, and Violence in the Hebrew Prophets* (Minneapolis: Fortress, 1995) 103.

Feminist critics have highlighted numerous biblical narratives that depict violence done to women. Examples include Hagar (Genesis 16, 21), Tamar (2 Samuel 13), Jezebel (2 Kings 9:30-37), and the Levite's wife (Judges 19–21). These narratives were often bypassed by traditional commentators and religious leaders until feminists realized that the texts graphically expose women in unjust situations. In so doing, these critics have identified a "canon" within the canon of Scripture. Like the medieval rabbis, they select texts from within the tradition and use these texts to further their agenda.

The rabbis used the technique of "proof-texting" to support their interpretations of biblical narratives. In rabbinic scholarship the term "proof-texting" is used to refer to an internal manipulation of tradition to offer new interpretations. Feminist critique calls the entire biblical tradition into question by noting the fundamental patriarchal agenda inscribed in the text. What value, then, does the Bible hold for all humanity, including feminists? The Bible portrays the saga of real life, people with flaws and foibles, yet there is a voice, sometimes muted, but persistent, that calls us to justice and love.

## Commitment to Liberation

The biblical text and the medieval rabbis supported the traditions of the community of Israel. Feminist interests can and must go beyond national, religious, social, and ethnic boundaries. They are concerned with broader issues, such as women's relative anonymity in society and their powerlessness to direct their own lives. They are concerned with entrenched legal systems that do not respond to the need for change. They often eschew stereotypes of women as victims, obedient subjects, virgins, helpless maidens, and dependents. Feminism calls for a transformation rooted at a spiritual center that advocates justice, liberates the oppressed, affirms life, and promotes well-being.

Achieving the goal of liberation is not an easy task. Factions develop, voices go unheard, strategies vary, and political alliances shift. The process of liberation is an ongoing cycle of attentive listening, consciousness-raising, strategizing, action, and reflection. As new situations arise, the cycle begins again, but not from scratch. Each cycle builds on the experiences of past efforts.

## What Can the Rabbis Contribute to Feminism?

The medieval rabbis can enrich feminist critique through the literary form of midrash. While their own midrash may reflect attempts to bring justice to unjust circumstances, it is the women's potential use of the form that offers promise for today. (For example, in Chapter Three Judith Plaskow's midrash on Eve and Lilith offers an authentic modern feminist voice for a narrative long used to oppress women.) Modern feminist midrash offers an opportunity for direct engagement with biblical narratives resulting in a continuing dialogue about time-honored values. Ancient midrash, with its variety of opinions sometimes set side by side, can serve as a model for acknowledging the multiplicity of feminist voices. Further, rabbinic midrash informs our historical understanding of how values are reinterpreted over time. In the last chapter we will use the literary form of midrash to draw new meanings from Judges 11 to enhance our understanding of God and the complexity of human life.

## Summary

In this chapter we have proposed a conversation between the medieval rabbis and modern feminists on values. Both groups are concerned with justice, loyalty (love), compassion, and respect for tradition. The rabbis are informed by their own tradition and seek resolution within that framework, while the feminists take a broader view, recognizing the problem of patriarchal structures worldwide.

# CHAPTER SEVEN

*Modern Midrash—An Ongoing Dialogue*

Reading the Bible in the early twenty-first century poses a variety of problems. We understand it as a collection of writings from an ancient people living in a culture far removed from our own. We know little about that culture and virtually nothing about the writers themselves, but we do recognize intriguing characters who act more or less like ourselves. We probably know submissive women like Jephthah's daughter, arrogant and trapped men like Jephthah, and absent mothers of abused girls. We are prone to criticize women who return to abusers, men who lack imaginative solutions to problems, and a culture of war that destroys families. The ancient stories are really our own stories.

Midrashic criticism and feminist interpretation help us bridge the gap between the narrative of Jephthah's daughter and the modern world. The rabbis kept the text alive by highlighting injustices with imaginative story. Feminist interpreters uncovered the patriarchal framework of the narrative, exposing the hierarchical structure of religious and social systems in general. Both interpretative strategies invite dialogue between the reader and the text.

In this final chapter we will bring our interpretative task full circle, asking modern readers to interact with Judges 11 by composing their own "midrash." Contributors to this chapter were first trained in historical and literary aspects of the Bible. They were asked to identify narrative silences in the text using the close reading strategies described in Chapter One. They were then asked to write imaginative midrash that was limited only by the general outline, major characters, and general progression of the story. They were also expected to maintain the theology of monotheism and the role of God in the history of Israel. New characters could be introduced and old characters could be expanded.

Narrative silences in biblical stories invite speculation as to what motivates characters to act as they do. Contributors identify these narrative silences and position their midrash in the gaps. They also bring their own values to the text as they attempt to explain the behavior of the biblical characters. Thus by its nature modern midrash is self-revelatory, exposing the values of the writers, as was true of the rabbis and the feminists in their critiques.

This chapter is a collaborative enterprise of my students and colleagues. It is an interactive effort to find meaning in a violent story set within a canon of sacred texts. The writers represent wide-ranging viewpoints and life experiences. Their ranks include African-Americans, Israelis, males, females, Christians, Jews, and those unaffiliated with any religion. Together their conversation weaves a tapestry that makes the story of Jephthah's daughter relevant for today. Their midrash suggests that some have experienced the loss of a mother or had a difficult relationship with a mother; some loved their fathers, some were acquainted with abuse, and some found solace in the company of other women. Some were more concerned with position within the family, some were young and wildly romantic, some were cynical about the dream of justice, and some were mothers and grandmothers who wanted a smoother path for their offspring.

Contributors to this chapter include students at Edgewood College, undergraduates and master's degree candidates, my daughter, and friends who were intrigued with this project. All gave consent for the use of their work and agreed to appropriate editing. They are listed here in alphabetical order to allow their work to remain anonymous: Yaerit Aharon, Liz Allen, Gloria Alt, Brooke Anderson, Maytee Aspuro, Reyna Collura, Valerie Cappozzo, Christine Cassata, Tracey Corder, Charles Davis, Susan Hansen, Teri Jo Hill, Lorin Johnson, David Kordell, Ann Krummel, Sarah Leiser, Eliza Leitzinger, C. J. Love, Sarah MacLeod, Kim Marshall, Richard Parker, K. Ritchie Rheaume, Alicia Siebers, Lauren Todd, and Karen Wagner.

## The Task: Creating New Midrash

The contributors followed a four-step process in preparing their midrash. First, they located narrative silences in the Jephthah story by color coding the text, following the guidelines presented in Chapter One. Second, paying special attention to marginalized characters, they retold the story from the point of view of each character in order to see the text anew. They were cautioned not to attribute motivations or emotions not strictly stated in the narrative. Third, they each wrote a midrash that filled in a gap, as described above. Fourth, they analyzed their midrash by paying particular attention to the values they brought to their writing and how these values related to social, political, and religious issues. The student contributors shared their midrash and analyses in class.

The purpose of this exercise was to learn to read ancient stories through the lens of changing cultural and political circumstances in order to gain new perspectives, pose strategies for change, and interact in community. I have grouped the resulting midrashim to reflect themes articulated by the writers. The categories concern relationships between mothers and daughters, fathers and daughters, and among women, in addition to assessments of Jephthah's emotional state, the annual ceremony, and the nature of God. Multiple voices are reflected under each theme, creating a new conversation about Jephthah's daughter.

## Mother and Daughter

The modern midrashic writers quoted in this section are concerned with the relationship between the daughter and her (missing) mother. One writer deals with the missing mother by proposing that she died prior to the events recorded in Judges 11:

> The mother died before she had to suffer the violent death of her only daughter. At least she did not see the virgin blood poured out upon the stone and her husband wielding the sacrificial knife. Nor did the mother hear her husband blame his child for his own guilt.

The mother is spared knowledge of her daughter's fate, but the narrator does not spare the reader the ugly details of the young woman's death, which not only convict Jephthah but also emphasize how lonely the daughter was in death.

Another attempt to explain the mother's absence imagines that the mother had betrayed her husband and Jephthah had sent her away to live in shame. In this case the daughter knew her mother's whereabouts and spent the two months on the mountain with her. "What brings you here to me, daughter?" asks her mother. "Father is making me a burnt offering for the LORD." Her mother counsels: "Do not run away, daughter. I do not want you to live in shame as I do." This mother considers death a worthier fate than living in shame. She seems to share the same fate as Jephthah's own mother, who is only described as a prostitute in the biblical story.

Other writers have the mother present to the story. Mother and daughter prepare a feast to celebrate Jephthah's return. Seeing him in the distance, the mother sends the daughter out to greet him. The mother follows with the food for the celebration and overhears her husband's words to her daughter. She embraces her daughter and rebukes Jephthah: "How dare you! I will not allow you to sacrifice our only heir. Go back to the LORD and offer another sacrifice in her place." Jephthah trembles at his wife's words but refuses to heed them. After the daughter leaves for the mountains, the mother falls to her knees and begs the LORD to dismiss the vow. She blames herself for sending her daughter out of the house and then pleads that the LORD will accept her as the sacrifice. She grabs her husband's knife and proclaims to Jephthah, "I am to be your sacrifice to the LORD." She drives the knife into her heart and falls to the ground dead at the entrance to their tent. In this midrash the mother confronts her husband, confronts the LORD, and, failing to get a satisfactory response, offers her own life. The nurturing mother in this midrash will stop at nothing to protect her child.

A variation on this midrash has the mother rebuking Jephthah:

> You sacrificed our innocent child for your own glory of wartime victory. We are your family, your daughter is from your own flesh. Is your love for her not dearer to you than the approval of men who once hated you and drove you from your father's house? Take my life instead, sparing our beloved daughter. Surely the LORD will accept this exchange.

The mother's fierce love for her child supercedes allegiance to her husband, the nation, and God.

In yet another midrash the mother and daughter discuss issues pertaining to the laws about vows. After the daughter consents to the sacrifice she seeks comfort from her mother. The mother is filled with confusion and grief, saying:

> Is it not true that our God does not delight in human sacrifice? How then could your father have made such a vow? Why didn't he wait for a sign of God's approval before he allowed you to seal it with your consent?

The daughter urges her mother not to speak out against her father because she has already given consent and does not wish to bring God's wrath upon her family's house. This entire conversation takes place between the two women. Jephthah, who might be persuaded to revoke the vow, is not consulted. In fact, the daughter fears God's wrath if the issue is taken to Jephthah. The family dynamic is avoidance of confrontation even in grave circumstances. For the rest of her life the mother wonders if the sacrifice was pleasing to God and whether she should have interfered as her heart told her to do. She finally realizes that the will of God is not necessarily revealed in the law or the keeping of the law, but in one's own heart.

In this same midrash the mother raises key criticisms pertaining to the making and keeping of vows. She introduces the idea of God giving a sign that the vow was legitimate and that the daughter's consent was necessary to seal the vow. The author begs for God's interference and judgment while giving the daughter an elevated status before the law. The mother comes to know that God works through insights within the human heart. The midrash leaves the reader uneasy. Perhaps the mother could have saved her daughter if she had trusted her own insight.

One midrash has the mother's presence framing the daughter's departure to the mountains and her return. With her mother's blessing and guidance, the daughter and her friends wander the mountains praying and listening to God. The waiting mother greets her when she returns. Here the mother and God complement each other in caring for the daughter.

Another scenario has the mother taking revenge on Jephthah. After Jephthah carries out his sacrifice, the mother refuses to bear him any more children. Her punishment strikes at the heart of his concern about having heirs.

The mothers depicted here are nurturers with some of them willing to confront Jephthah, and even God, in an appeal for justice. There is no peaceful resolution to the conflict. Imaginative solutions are precluded by rigid ideas about keeping vows.

## Father and Daughter

A number of the modern midrashic writers claim that the daughter loved her father. Her immediate consent to his vow indicates her love. For example, one midrash gives reasons for her blind devotion. In the absence of the mother, Jephthah taught his daughter the skills necessary to run the household and ensure their livelihood when he was at war. On another occasion, one writer proposes, Jephthah secured her safety after she had been raped, by sparing her public humiliation and death. She loves her father and honors him for his wisdom.

Nonverbal communication between father and daughter signifies a range of emotional response. When he arrives home he does not open his arms to receive her, and she sees a great sadness in his eyes, followed by a flash of anger, as she hears his blaming words. As a daughter living in troubled times she understands the warrior culture and weeps for him and the grief she knows he feels. Upon her return from the mountains she sees his cold brooding eyes and his hardened heart. At this moment her hope vanishes.

In other cases writers imagine various conversations between father and daughter. In one she responds to her father, "Is it my fault that you made the vow? Renounce your vow!" He defends himself with "I expected that an animal, a guard, or a slave would be the first living thing to come forth from my house." At this point Jephthah turns on her, revealing a darker side to his personality: "Because you have made me miserable and wretched, you will be the victim of my vow." Jephthah's vindictive nature makes it difficult to muster any sympathy for his plight.

On the other hand, Jephthah can be portrayed as a contrite man. His daughter asks, "Is the love you have for me that small, that you would just let me die? Can't you ask God to be merciful?" Jephthah replies, "My dear and only daughter, I am sorry for the vow I have made, but I cannot turn my back on the LORD. You know I love you, but I made a promise that I must keep." In this version Jephthah exhibits no guile; he is a sad and confused man.

Another contributor imagines the daughter's bewilderment at hearing her father's blame. It sparks her adolescent spirit of independence and search for self-identity. She flees to the mountains, shouldering the burden of her senseless fate alone, apart from her family. As she walks the road of independence she turns her back on her family and finds support among her peers. Surely her friends will understand.

The emboldened daughter who is able to call her father to account for his actions must have experienced strength from another source. Perhaps the Spirit of the LORD came upon her as it had come upon her father before he went into battle. Maybe the spirit gave her the inner wisdom to protest:

> My father, when our ancestors were about to enter the Promised Land, God gave them a choice: "I set before you life and death, blessing and curse. Choose life so that your descendants may live." I appeal to you to choose life for me and blessings for yourself.

We might also imagine that Jephthah sought God's guidance, as in this writer's account in which, overcome with grief, Jephthah goes into the wilderness. There the Spirit of the LORD comes to him, saying:

> By promising a burnt sacrifice like the people who worship foreign gods you have broken the covenant I made with your ancestor Abraham. Therefore you shall not be blessed with descendents as Abraham

was so blessed; and your only daughter, whom you love, shall remain a virgin.

Jephthah does not gain the insight that Abraham acquired on the mountain, and his line is cut off.

Another twist on the story imagines that when Jephthah arrives home he sees both his daughter and a faithful slave who has been a consolation to him in the past. He must decide which of the two to sacrifice. His daughter says: "Look into your heart; the answer lies within you." As he is about to announce his decision, his daughter cries out again, "Let it be me, for I know your slave is a comfort to you." Jephthah acquiesces to his daughter's request and honors his vow. The daughter's heroics and willingness to take the servant's place betray her lack of self-esteem.

In some accounts Jephthah's daughter chastises her father for failing to seek other means of carrying out his vow. Other writers explain that her fear and awe of God motivate her consent.

The emotions related in the foregoing midrash are summarized in this entry. Imagine a relationship made up not only of love but also obedience, honor, fear, and duty. Surely her father's spirit is present with her on the mountain as much as when the two of them were physically under the same roof. She belongs to him—in his eyes, in the eyes of her village, and, sadly, in her own eyes.

## The Women Tell It on the Mountain

Our modern storytellers imagine the gathering on the mountain as a time for sharing advice, strategizing for justice, and mourning the impending death of a loved one. The first example picks up the narrative after Jephthah tells his daughter that yes, she may go the mountains for two months.

When the daughter tells her story to her companions, they offer her advice that could save her life:

One step outside her father's gate the first friend says to her, "Now run, that you may be beyond the reach of harm!" And she says, "Where shall I live in warmth and sustenance and meaning, even if I do not die by violence?" And her friend turns from her and goes back.

Two weeks outside her father's gate the second friend says to her, "Seek then a writ of protection from the court, that the hand of an abuser will be stayed by a greater authority." And she says, "Shall I make my shame public, inviting the scrutiny of strangers?" And her friend turns from her and goes back.

Ten weeks outside her father's gate the third friend says to her, "Surely you will not return." And she says, "Perhaps my absence has brought change and has remedied this man's belief. Clearly, no other choice but love's own hope lies before me." And her friend says, "You are a fool," and goes back.

The daughter fails to help herself. Perhaps she could have sought refuge with a relative in another clan, or she could have sought legal protection. Instead, she is under the illusion that her father will see the error of his ways and change his mind.

During the long cool nights she wonders how she might survive alone. Perhaps she could become a servant ministering at the shrine at Shiloh. Or she could pose as an orphan and receive special gifts of food. If all else fails she could become a prostitute and live independently, like Rahab. If she ran away, perhaps her father would drag her back, as the Levite had done with his wife. As she explores these possibilities she comes to realize how limited her life as an independent woman would be.

Several midrash writers envision the time on the mountain as a consciousness-raising period during which the women come to understand their oppression in patriarchal society. One suggests that the daughter joins a group of women who were already working to change social injustices. In this group she finds that her experience enables her to speak with great knowledge and passion, and she discovers that she can forgive the one who sought to harm her. Within the group she learns to heal discord and is known for her wisdom. Other women who have been silenced for too long join the growing movement for peace and justice. The passion the daughter experiences during the two months enables her to have hope that her father will change his mind. Alas, she discovers the world could not be changed in such a short time.

Other contributors saw the time on the mountain as a time of mourning and grief. When the women arrive on the mountain they find a small cave in the rock that will give them protection and they build a fire to keep warm in the cool of the night. The daughter longs for the embrace of a mother she never knew and yearns to embrace the child she will never have. This portrayal emphasizes the daughter's need to be nurtured and to nurture. In other words, "I lament the husband who will never know me, my barren womb that will not produce offspring, and the tomorrow that I will never experience. My life passes like a shadow ending all my days."

The daughter prays:

> O God of our fathers, look with mercy on your faithful daughter. My pitiful life has been promised to you in exchange for the great victory you have given to your people. I stand before you, insignificant and obedient. But turmoil fills my heart. I have never honored you with sons. Deny this vow of my father and spare the life of your servant. I bow to you, O God of Abraham. Hear my prayer and save your daughter.

In this prayer three fathers are invoked. God, as father of the people, and Abraham, the father who avoids sacrificing his son, offer a contrast to her father who will sacrifice his child. The daughter calls herself pitiful and insignificant, leaving open the thought that it is really her father who truly embodies these characteristics.

Perhaps the time on the mountain resembles the Jewish mourning custom called "shiva." After the funeral of a loved one, the family of the deceased remains at home for seven days. Friends bring food and offer a daily prayer. The women on the mountain could have brought special foods, lamented, and offered comfort to Jephthah's daughter.

One midrash writer speculates that the daughter becomes suicidal. Fearing that she might take her own life, the women take turns keeping vigil with her. Her state of mind is graphically described. During the two months her sullen mood turns to anger. She cries out to God, asking why her father made such a vow. Her companions fail in their attempts to comfort her. For days she acts like one crazed—calling out to God, calling on the spirit of her mother whom she never knew, cursing her father, whom she had loved, for making the cruel and foolish vow he made, refusing food and drink, and bewailing her future. She becomes delirious with misery, begging that she join her mother in death. At that moment the rock she is standing on breaks loose and she falls with a resounding cry that echoes throughout the land. Her companions run to the edge of the cliff where their friend has fallen to her death. The women gather flowers and place them on that spot to honor her. At home in Mizpah, Jephthah hears the wailing cry of his daughter. When her companions return, he falls on his knees. He goes to the mountain to grieve the loss of his daughter. There he builds an altar and offers sacrifices to God in honor of his only daughter, whom he loved.

In this midrash the daughter's despair ends not in suicide but in a death caused by cosmic forces. The cosmos responds in a cry that falls upon Jephthah's ears. He can do nothing less than offer a more pleasing sacrifice to God on that very mountain.

The mood of impending tragedy is captured in this midrash: Imagine singing of loss throughout all those hot and desolate days, and crouching in the darkness all those nights, watching the moon change, knowing that the time to return was coming closer.

The biblical narrative is completely silent regarding the time spent on the mountain. The silence mutes any call for social change. The daughter's death seals the silence. The voice of mourning might be more easily imagined in the biblical story, given the reference to the annual ceremony to honor the daughter.

## The Daughter Is Not Sacrificed

The biblical narrative states that at the end of two months the daughter returned to her father, who did with her according to the vow he had made. Like the medieval sage David Kimhi, modern midrash writers imagine that, however Jephthah fulfilled his vow, he did not kill his daughter. A romantic view imagines that she found a lover among the shepherds. One of her friends is so happy for her that she convinces the daughter to change places with her. The friend returns, wearing the daughter's clothing and veiling her face. In his distress Jephthah fails to recognize that the girl is not his daughter and offers her as the sacrifice. Another view has the daughter begging her father to sacrifice a servant in her place. In these stories the daughter has more value than her substitute, especially when the substitute is a servant.

In another instance the father runs out to greet the daughter as she returns. In her absence God has spoken to him in a dream, telling him to spare his daughter and slaughter a sheep instead.

## Jephthah the Man

In an attempt to understand Jephthah's behavior modern writers imagine what his home life was like. One midrash, told from the point of view of a friend, relates that Jephthah's mother beguiled Jephthah's father and bore him a son. Gilead was pleased with the child's strength, which indicated that the boy was destined to become a mighty warrior. After Gilead's wife bore him legitimate sons he turned aside from his firstborn, just as Abraham had turned from Ishmael. Jephthah never got over the loss of his father's esteem. He took greater risks and made foolish boasts to win his father's approval. Once he made a promise, he never backed down from it. He could not bear to be a failure in the eyes of his friends and fellow warriors.

Jephthah was clever in his negotiations with the Ammonites. He stated Israel's case as well as any prophet. The victory over the Ammonites went to Jephthah's head. In making the vow he seemed to think that it would increase his stature with the tribe if he proved his piety. He was a gambler who could not see the folly of his vow. He did not see that God would not require a child's life as the price of a military victory.

Another version portrays a conspiracy perpetrated by Jephthah's half brothers. Fearing that Gilead would restore Jephthah's inheritance once victory was won, the brothers scheme to have his daughter be the first to greet him. Jephthah would be forced to carry out his vow or suffer shame before his father, the tribe, and God. In this way Jephthah was tricked by his brothers and entrapped by his own pride.

A slightly different twist explaining the circumstance of Jephthah's vow claims that Jephthah's bold vow in full view of his fellow warriors increased his stature before his army. However, if he had been alone with the LORD he would have spoken more directly from his heart.

Each of these midrash writers empathizes with Jephthah's plight. Jephthah acted as he did because of a troubled childhood. He is constantly trying to prove himself worthy in the eyes of others.

In contrast to attempts to excuse Jephthah, one writer expresses graphic anger toward him: "Was ever a burnt offering less pleasing to God? Jephthah may wail and rend his garments all he wants. I, for one, will never feel sorry for a murderer. Would that the Ammonites had slain him and sent his head back on a pole!"

## The Tradition of the Annual Ceremony

Feminist interpretation suggests two possibilities for the annual four-day ceremony commemorating Jephthah's daughter. It could be a rite of passage marking the transition to womanhood or it could be a mourning ceremony.

The women gathered for the days just before and just after the new moon. As the moon waned to darkness they met in a mountain cave to mourn their sister. Young women, pregnant women, women with children at the breast, and women past childbearing keened laments as they retold the story of the girl's life and death. They recalled those who died in childbirth, those who miscarried, and the children who died. In the dark of the new moon they told secret stories of goddesses who insured fertility with potions, amulets, and incantations. As a sliver of the new moon emerged they brought out scented oils for anointing, sweet cakes, wine, and ribbons to weave in each other's hair. Their mourning turned to a celebration of their fruitful bodies and the joy of children.

One writer imagines girls and women rushing to the mountain place where Jephthah's daughter had fled. They pull their hair and chant: "How long, O LORD, must we endure? How long will men puff themselves up in pride? How long will they contend that you, O LORD, condone their wars and their killing?" The girls weave garlands of flowers symbolizing the children the daughter did not bear.

Another midrash has the women gathering in a holy space, a temple in the trees. They build an altar from the stones they gather and offer appropriate sacrifices of grain and oil. They share stories of courage, poems of love, and memories of their beloved friend.

One version celebrates the daughter as a martyr to the cause of justice for women. The women gather in solidarity to share stories and strategize for rights within their tribe. The movement grows and spreads throughout the land and continues to the present day. In another case a radical voice emerges, accusing the women for their preoccupation with bearing children. "Is that our only value? Your acceptance keeps us in this role. Why don't we protest the deeper reasons that led to our friend's death?"

The focus of these ceremonies is the bonding of women through shared experience, from which subversive activity for justice emerges.

## God

In the modern midrash God is depicted as having a range of involvement in the narrative. God may orchestrate each action, control some action, or stand to the side as the narrative unfolds.

In one example God is displeased with Jephthah's vow because it is self-serving. Jephthah must be punished, and that will be accomplished through the death of his daughter. God directs her to greet her father and affirms her consent to be a sacrifice. God predestines her to be a sacrifice for her father's foolish vow.

Another midrash imagines the mother interceding with God: "She is my only child; why must he offer our child as a burnt offering?" God replies by reminding her that God kept God's part of the bargain by granting victory and Jephthah has to keep his word by fulfilling the vow. In this example God both models and demands fulfillment of an obligation.

For some writers God is upheld as a God of compassion, justice, and love. Thus God weeps with the women on the mountain, mourns over Jephthah's lack of wisdom, and suffers when the daughter is sacrificed.

Another response challenges God's absence. Some of the women talk secretly of blaming God, but God has no part in this travesty. "Whose command was it that slaughtered this child? He should have named his child 'Rachel,' that is, 'ewe,' for she was treated in the end no better than a dumb sheep." While anger is directed against Jephthah, it might be more appropriately turned toward God.

These few responses to God's role in Judg 11:29-40 are a microcosm of theologies about the nature of God. The narrative permits every view, from predestination to a God who allows the human drama to unfold without divine interference. The question of unjust suffering is raised but remains unresolved.

## The Value of Modern Midrash

In this compilation of modern midrash we have engaged in an interactive method of biblical interpretation. Contributors have spoken from their own social locations and experiences in their conversation with Judges 11. They have upheld the values of family love and loyalty while recognizing the complexity of human relationships. Not all mothers and fathers succeed in protecting their children. Not all families respect each other's voices and concerns, and tragedy can result.

Our writers wrestle with concepts of individuality and community. They are outraged that the daughter has no control over her fate and that she dies alone. They speak eloquently of her internal grief. However, the time on the mountain is also a time of community-building among the women as they offer advice, explore alternatives, strategize for justice, and support each other.

The role of God in human suffering remains elusive in the midrash entries. The hidden nature of God is as mysterious as it was at the beginning of this task, but we have had an opportunity to engage in a conversation with ancient and modern voices, sharing our experiences of this text with each other. In the process we see that there are no simple solutions and there is no one way to read a text. However, through dialogue with the biblical text we can come to a better understanding of ourselves, each other, and God.

## Conclusion

In this book we have brought together medieval rabbis, feminist biblical scholars, and current readers in a conversation about a narrative of a young woman who is sacrificed to God by her father. We have noted the difficulties in dating the writing and editing of the Judges 11 story, which is set in pre-monarchial Israel. Social issues, such as the nature of a vow, the practice of human sacrifice, and the role of women in ancient Israel, inform an understanding of this text. As the Spirit of the LORD, God insures military victory and is the one to whom vows are made, but God is also the one who does not intercede to save Jephthah's daughter. The plight of the daughter and the apparent absence of God motivate medieval rabbis and modern feminists to postulate new meanings for this text. The rabbis are concerned primarily with justice within patriarchal Judaism while feminists are concerned with patriarchal social systems worldwide. The rabbis construct their critique in the form of midrash as story told within the gaps of the biblical story. Feminists position the woman of the narrative at the center of their inquiry and analyze how she relates to the patriarchal systems of domination.

Conversation between the rabbis and feminists is possible because they are probing the same issues—justice, compassion, loyalty, and the nature of God. New voices enrich this conversation as each generation discovers its values and dreams for the future in the ongoing story.

This book closes with an invitation to the reader. Become intimately involved with the possibilities of biblical narrative. Do the historical and literary homework first. Check out what others have said about the text over time. Then bring your experience to the text in a dialogue with others. Explore the possibilities that arise for transforming society. Then let us join Judith Plaskow in her midrash as Eve and Lilith "return to the garden, bursting with possibilities, ready to rebuild it together."[1]

---

[1] Judith Plaskow, "A Jewish Feminist Midrash on Lilith and Eve," in Rosemary Radford Ruether, ed., *Womanguides: Readings Toward a Feminist Theology* (Boston: Beacon, 1985) 74.

# APPENDIX
## *Midrash Through the Ages*

This appendix contains excerpts from rabbinic midrash, an example of medieval poetry, and a modern poem on Jephthah's daughter. Since many of these texts are not easily accessible, they are included here. I have attempted to arrange them in chronological order, relying on dating information that is far from conclusive.

### Pseudo-Philo 40 (first century C.E.)[1]

*And Jephthah came and attacked the sons of Ammon, and the* LORD *delivered them into his hands, and he struck down* sixty of their *cities.* And Jephthah returned *in peace,* and women came out *to meet him in song and dance. And it was his only daughter who came out* of the house first in the dance *to meet* her father. *And* when *Jephthah saw her, he grew faint and said,* "Rightly was your name called Seila, that you might be offered in sacrifice. And now who will put my heart in the balance and my soul on the scale? And I will stand by and see which will win out, whether it is the rejoicing that has occurred or the sadness that befalls me. And because *I opened my mouth to* my LORD in song with vows, "I *cannot* call that back again."

*And* Seila *his daughter said to him,* "And who is there who would be sad in death, seeing the people freed? Or do you not remember what happened in the days of our fathers when the father placed the son as a holocaust, and he did not refuse him but gladly gave consent to him, and the one being offered was ready and one who was offering was rejoicing? And now do not annul everything you have vowed, but carry it out. Yet one request I ask of you before I die, a small demand I seek before I give back my

[1] Text in italics corresponds to Judges 11. From James H. Charlesworth, ed., *The Old Testament Pseudepigrapha* (Garden City, NY: Doubleday, 1985) 2:353. The punctuation, spelling, and grammar in this Appendix are as given in the English translations cited.

soul: that *I may go into the mountains and stay* in the hills and walk among the rocks, *I and my virgin companions,* and I will pour out my tears there and tell of the sadness of my youth. And the trees of the field will weep for me, and the beasts of the field will lament over me. For I am not sad because I am to die nor does it pain me to give back my soul, but because my father was caught up in the snare of his vow; and if I did not offer myself willingly for sacrifice, I fear that my death would not be acceptable or I would lose my life in vain. These things I will tell on the mountains, and afterward I will return." *And* her father *said, "Go."*

And Seila the daughter of Jephthah, she and her virgin companions, *went out* and came and told it to the wise men of the people, and no one could respond to her word. And afterward she came to Mount Stelac, and the LORD thought of her by night and said, "Behold now I have shut up the tongue of the wise men of my people for this generation so that they cannot respond to the daughter of Jephthah, to her word, in order that my word be fulfilled and my plan that I thought out not be foiled. And I have seen that the virgin is wise in contrast to her father and perceptive in contrast to all the wise men who are here. And now let her life be given at his request, and her *death* will be *precious before* me always, and she will go away and fall into the bosom of her mothers."

And when the daughter of Jephthah came to Mount Stelac, she began to weep, and this is her lamentation that she lamented and wept over herself before she departed. And she said,

> Hear, you mountains, my lamentation;
> and pay attention, you hills, to the tears of my eyes;
> and be witness, you rocks, of the weeping of my soul.
> Behold how I am put to the test!
> But not in vain will my life be taken away.
> May my words go forth in the heavens,
> and my tears be written in the firmament!
> That a father did not refuse the daughter, whom he had sworn to sacrifice,
> that a ruler granted that his only daughter be promised for sacrifice.
> But I have not made good on my marriage chamber,
> and I have not retrieved my wedding garlands.
> For I have not been clothed in splendor while sitting in my woman's chamber,
> And I have not used the sweet-smelling ointment,
> And my soul has not rejoiced in the oil of anointing that has been prepared for me.
> O Mother, in vain have you borne your only daughter,

because Sheol has become my bridal chamber,
and on earth there is only my woman's chamber.
And may all the blend of oil that you have prepared for me be poured
    out,
and the white robe that my mother has woven, the moth will eat it.
And the crown of flowers that my nurse plaited for me for the festival,
may it wither up;
And the coverlet that she wove of hyacinth and purple in my woman's
    chamber,
may the worm devour it.
And may my virgin companions tell of me in sorrow and weep for me
through the days.
You trees, bow down your branches and weep over my youth.
You beasts of the forests, come and bewail my virginity,
for my years have been cut off
and the time of my life grown old in darkness.

And on saying these things Seila *returned to her father, and he did everything that he had vowed* and offered the holocausts. Then all the virgins of Israel gathered together and buried the daughter of Jephthah and wept for her. And the children of Israel made a great lamentation and established that in that month on the fourteenth day of the month they should come together every year and weep for Jephthah's daughter for four days. And they named her tomb in keeping with her name: Seila.

*And Jephthah judged* the sons of *Israel* ten *years, and he died and was buried* with his fathers.

## Josephus, *Antiquities of the Jews* 5.7.10 (first century C.E.)[2]

And when he had given them this answer, he sent the ambassadors away. And when he had prayed for victory and vowed to perform sacred offices, and if he came home in safety, to offer in sacrifice what living creature [who]soever should first meet him; he joined battle with the enemy and gained a great victory, and in his pursuit slew the enemies all along as far as the city Minnith. He then passed over to the land of the Ammonites, and overthrew many of their cities, and took their prey, and freed his own people from that slavery which they had undergone for eighteen years. But

[2] Josephus, *Antiquities of the Jews,* in *The Works of Josephus,* trans. William Whiston (Peabody, MA: Hendrickson, 1987) 144. *Antiquities* is not classified as a midrash. Josephus is writing a history of the Jews beginning at creation, relying on the biblical narrative but including his own opinions.

as he came back, he fell into a calamity no way correspondent to the great actions he had done; for it was his daughter that came to meet him; she was also an only child and a virgin: upon this Jephthah heavily lamented the greatness of his affliction, and blamed his daughter for being so forward in meeting him, for he had vowed to sacrifice her to God. However, this action that was to befall her was not ungrateful to her, since she should die upon the occasion of her father's victory, and the liberty of her fellow citizens: she only desired her father to give her leave for two months, to bewail her youth with her fellow citizens; and then she agreed, that at the aforementioned time he might do with her according to his vow. Accordingly, when that time was over, he sacrificed his daughter as a burnt offering . . . such an oblation as was neither conformable to the law nor acceptable to God, not weighing with himself what opinion the hearers would have of such a practice.

### *Genesis Rabbah* 60.3 (fourth century)[3]

"Behold, I am standing by the spring of water, and the daughters of the men of the city are coming out to draw water. Let the maiden to whom I shall say, 'Pray let down your jar that I may drink,' and who shall say, 'Drink, and I will water your camels'—let her be the one whom you have appointed for your servant Isaac. By this I shall know that you have shown steadfast love to my master" (Gen 24:13-14).

Four asked for what they wanted in an improper way. To three what they asked was given in a proper way, and to the fourth what was asked was not given in the proper way.

These are they: Eliezer, Caleb, Saul, and Jephthah.

Eliezer: "Let the maiden to whom I shall say, 'Pray let down your jar that I may drink,' and who shall say, 'Drink, and I will water your camels'—let her be the one whom you have appointed for your servant Isaac. By this I shall know that you have shown steadfast love to my master" (Gen 24:13-14).

[What made this statement improper?] Would that apply even to a serving girl? But the Holy One, blessed be he, designated Rebecca for him, so in a proper way he gave him what he had asked.

Caleb: "And Caleb said, 'Whoever smites Kiriath Sepher and takes it, to him will I give Achsah, my daughter, as wife" (Josh 15:16).

---

[3] Jacob Neusner, *Genesis Rabbah: The Judaic Commentary to the Book of Genesis* (Atlanta: Scholars, 1985) 2:315–17. See also *Genesis Rabbah,* trans. H. Freedman and Maurice Simon (London: Soncino, 1939) 2:526–28.

Is it possible that he would give her even to a slave? The Holy One, blessed be he, designated Othniel for him.

Saul: "And the men of Israel said, 'Have you seen this man who has come up? Surely he has come up to defy Israel, and the man who kills him the king will enrich with great riches and will give him his daughter'" (1 Sam 17:25).

Is it possible that he would give her even to a slave? The Holy One, blessed be he, designated David for him.

Jephthah asked not in a proper way, and it was not in a proper way that the Holy One, blessed be he, responded to him.

He asked not in a proper way, as it is said, "Jephthah made a vow to the LORD and said, 'If you will give the Ammonites into my hand, then whoever comes forth from the doors of my house to meet me when I return victorious from the Ammonites shall be the LORD's and I will offer him up for a burnt offering'" (Judg 11:30-31).

Said to him the Holy One, blessed be he, "If a camel or an ass or a dog should come forth from your house, would you then offer him up as a burnt offering before me?"

What did the Holy One, blessed be he, do to him?

He responded to him not in a proper way and designated his daughter, as it is said, "Then Jephthah came to his home at Mizpah, and behold, his daughter came out to meet him with timbrels and with dances; she was his only child; beside her he had neither son nor daughter. And when he saw her, he tore his clothes and said, 'Alas my daughter, you have brought me very low and you have become the cause of great trouble to me'" (Judg 11:34-35).

R. Yohanan and R. Simeon b. Laqish: R. Yohanan said, "He was liable to pay off his statement of sanctification by paying the monetary worth involved."

R. Simeon b. Laqish said, "He was not even liable to pay off his statement on sanctification by paying the monetary worth involved."

"For we learned in the Mishnah: "If one has made a statement concerning an unclean beast or a beast that was blemished and unfit for the altar, 'Lo, this one is in the status of a burnt-offering,' he has said nothing, 'Lo, this is for the purpose of a burnt-offering,' then the thing is to be sold and a burnt offering purchased with the proceeds" (*m.Temurah* 5:6)."

But was Phinehas not there, who could have released him from his vow?

Phinehas said, "Lo, he needs me, and should I go to him? And not only so, but I am high priest and the son of a high priest, and should I go to an ordinary person?"

Jephthah said, "I am the head of the rulers of Israel, and should I go to Phinehas?"

[Due to the stubbornness of] this one and that one, the girl perished.

In a proverb people say, "Between the midwife and the woman in travail, the poor woman's baby is going to die."

Both of them, therefore, were punished on account of her blood.

Jephthah's limbs fell off of him limb by limb, and he therefore was buried in many places. That is in line with the following verse of scripture: "And Jephthah died and was buried in the cities of Gilead" (Judg 12:7). What is written is not, "in a city of Gilead" but rather, "In the cities of Gilead." [This teaches that a limb would fall off from him here and was buried where it fell, and a limb would fall off of him in another place and was buried where it fell.]

From Phinehas the Holy Spirit was taken away, as it is said, "Phinehas, the son of Eleazar, was ruler over them; in times past the LORD was with him" (1 Chr 9:20). What is written is not, ". . . is ruler over them," but rather, ". . . was ruler over them, i.e., in times past."

He had been with him in times past, but not now.


### *Song of Songs Rabbah* 3:8 (fourth century)[4]

"Leaping upon the mountains, bounding over the hills": the word "mountains" refers only to courts, in line with this usage: "I will depart and go down upon the mountains" (Judg 11:37).


### *Leviticus Rabbah* 37:4 (fifth century)[5]

This midrash is similar to *Genesis Rabbah* 60.3 with the exceptions noted below. In the case of Eliezer's request:

> Said the Holy One, blessed be He, to him: "If a Canaanite, slave girl, or a harlot had come out, would you still have said, 'Let the same be she that thou hast appointed for thy servant, even for Isaac'?"

---

[4] Jacob Neusner, *Introduction to Rabbinic Literature* (New York: Doubleday, 1994) 485.

[5] *Midrash Rabbah: Leviticus,* ed. H. Freedman and Maurice Simon (London: Soncino, 1939) 469.

In the case of Caleb's request:

> Said the Holy One, blessed be He: "If a Canaanite, or a bastard, or a slave had captured it, would you have given him to your daughter?"

In the case of Saul's request:

> Said the Holy One, blessed be He: "If an Ammonite, or a bastard, or a slave had killed him, would you have given him to your daughter?"

The midrash continues with Jephthah, Phinehas, and Jephthah's death, and the debate between the rabbis:

> R. Simeon b. Lakish and R. Johanan hold different opinions on his case. Resh Lakish says that he should have given money for her and offered a sacrifice bought with it upon the altar. R. Johanan says that he need not have given money, for we have learned that an animal that is fit to be offered on the altar should be offered, while one that is not fit to be offered on the altar should not be offered. Moreover, if anyone makes a vow and pays his vow, he will be privileged to pay his vow in Jerusalem.

## b. Baba Qamma 92b (sixth century)[6]

Whence can be derived the popular saying, "A bad date palm will make its way to a grove of barren trees?" . . . And there gathered themselves to Jephthah idle men and they went out with him. . . . In the Mishnah, "All that which is attached to an article that is subject to the law of defilement, will similarly become defiled. . . ."

## b. Ta'anit 4a (sixth century)[7]

Three [men] made haphazard requests, two of them were fortunate in the reply they received and one was not, namely, Eliezer, the servant of Abraham; Saul, the son of Kish; and Jephtha the Gileadite. Eliezer, the servant of Abraham, as it is written, So let it come to pass that the damsel,

---

[6] *Baba Qamma, The Babylonian Talmud,* trans. I. Epstein (London: Soncino, 1935) 536.

[7] *Ta'anit, The Babylonian Talmud,* trans. I. Epstein (London: Soncino, 1938) 10.

to whom I shall say, "Let down thy pitcher etc." She might have been lame or blind, but he was fortunate in the answer given to him in that Rebecca chanced to meet him. Saul, the son of Kish, as it is written, And it shall be, that the man who killeth him, the king will enrich him with great riches, and will give him his daughter. [He] might have been a slave or a bastard. He too was fortunate in that it chanced to be David. Jephthah, the Gileadite, as it is written, Then it shall be, that whatsoever cometh forth out of the doors of my house etc. It might have been an unclean thing. He, however, was fortunate in that it so happened that his own daughter came to meet him. This is what the prophet had in mind when he said to Israel, Is there no balm in Gilead? Is there no physician there? And it is further written, Which I commanded not, nor spake it, neither came it to my mind. "Which I commanded not": This refers to the sacrifice of the son of Mesha, the king of Moab, as it is said, Then he took his eldest son that should have reigned in his stead and offered him for a burnt offering. "Nor spake it." This refers to the daughter of Jephthah. "Neither came it to my mind": This refers to the sacrifice of Isaac, the son of Abraham.

### *Ecclesiastes Rabbah* (eighth century)[8]

"He was buried in the cities of Gilead" (Judg 12:7). In how many places, then, was he buried that it is stated, "He was buried in the cities of Gilead"? It teaches that each limb fell away from his body separately and was buried in its place [where it dropped off]. What loss did Phinehas sustain [as a punishment]? The Holy Spirit departed from him for two hundred years; for it is not written here "And Phinehas the son of Eleazar was ruler over them," but "And Phinehas the son of Eleazar was ruler over them in time past, the LORD being with him" (1 Chr 9:20).

### *Targum Jonathan of the Former Prophets*, Judg 11:29-40 (seventh to ninth century)[9]

And *a spirit of power from before the* LORD *resided* upon Jephthah, and he passed through Gilead and Manasseh, and he passed through Mizpah of Gilead and from Mizpah of Gilead he passed *unto* the sons of Ammon.

---

[8] *Midrash Rabbah: Ecclesiastes,* ed. H. Freedman and Maurice Simon (London: Soncino, 1939) 276.

[9] The text in italics is different from the biblical version. From *Targum Jonathan of the Former Prophets,* trans. Daniel J. Harrington and Anthony J. Saldarini (Wilmington: Michael Glazier, 1987) 82–83.

And Jephthah vowed a vow *before* the LORD, and said: "If indeed you give the sons of Ammon in my hand, whoever will come forth *outside* from the doors of my house to meet me when I return in peace from the sons of Ammon will be *before* the LORD, and I will offer him up as a holocaust." And Jephthah passed on to the sons of Ammon to *wage battle* against them, and the LORD gave them in his hand. And he struck them down from Aroer and unto the entrance of Minnith—twenty cities and unto *the plain of vineyards*, a very great slaughter. And the sons of Ammon were *shattered* from before the sons of Israel. And Jephthah came to Mizpah to his house. And behold his daughter came forth to meet him with timbrels and with dances. And she was his only child; besides her he had no son or daughter. And when he saw her, he tore his garments and said: "Woe, my daughter, indeed you have saddened me and you have become my grief, for I opened my mouth *in a vow before the* LORD and I cannot take it back." And she said to him: "Father, you have opened your mouth *in a vow before the* LORD. Do to me as it went forth from your mouth, after the LORD has worked for your retribution from your enemies, from the sons of Ammon." And she said to her father: "Let this thing be done to me. Leave me alone for two months, and I will go and *withdraw* upon the mountains and weep over my virginity, I and my companions." And he said, "Go." And he sent her away for two months, and she went, she and her companions, and she wept over her virginity upon the mountains. And at the end of two months she returned unto her father, and he did to her his vow that he vowed. And she did not know a man. And it was made a rule in Israel *in order that a man not offer up his son and his daughter for a holocaust as Jephthah the Gileadite did. And he was not inquiring of Phinehas the priest; and if he inquired of Phinehas the priest, he would have redeemed her with blood.* From time to time the daughters of Israel were going to lament the daughter of Jephthah the Gileadite four days in a year.

### *Tanhuma Be-hukkotai* 5,7 (ninth to tenth centuries)

Shulamit Valler translates the following passage:[10]

Thus it was with Jephthah the Gileadite, who because he was not a Torah scholar, lost his daughter when he was fighting Ammonites, in the hour when he made the vow: ". . . if thou shalt without fail deliver the children of Ammon into my hands, Then it shall be, that whatsoever

[10] Shulamit Valler, "The Story of Jephthah's Daughter in the Midrash," in Athalya Brenner, ed., *A Feminist Companion to Judges* (Sheffield: Sheffield Academic Press, 1999) 48–66, 55.

cometh forth of the doors of my house shall surely be the LORD's and I will offer it up for a burnt offering." In that hour the LORD was angry with him and he said, if a dog or a pig or a camel comes out of his house he would offer it up as a sacrifice to me? So he provided his daughter. Why? So that all who make vows will study the laws of pledges and oaths, and will not act mistakenly when they make vows.

The following passage was translated by William G. Braude in *The Book of Legends:* [11]

As Jephthah was making ready to offer up his daughter, she wept before him and pleaded, "My father, my father, I came out to meet you full of joy, and now you are about to slaughter me. Is it written in the Torah that Israel should offer the lives of their children upon the altar? Jephthah replied, "My daughter, I made a vow." She answered, "But Jacob our father vowed, 'Of all that Thou shalt give me I will surely give the tenth unto Thee' [Gen 28:22]. Then, when the Holy One gave him twelve sons, did he perchance offer one of them on an altar to the Holy One? Moreover, Hannah also vowed, 'I will give him unto the Lord all the days of his life' [1 Sam 1:11]—did she perchance offer her son [on an altar] to the Lord?"

Though she said all these things to him, Jephthah did not heed her, but he went up to the altar and slaughtered her before the Holy One.

At that moment, the Holy Spirit cried out in anguish: Have I ever asked you to offer living souls to Me? I commanded not, nor spoke it, neither came it into My mind [Jer 19:5].

### *Alphabet ben Sira* 4a-4b (eleventh century)[12]

In the vernal equinox God turned the waters of Egypt into blood and from that time on every year, at the time when the vernal equinox takes place, a drop of blood is thrown into the waters, which poisons them. The same thing happens at the summer solstice, the time when Moses smote the rock, and blood began to flow therefrom; at the autumnal equinox, the time when Abraham stretched out his hand to slay Isaac and the knife began to bleed; at the winter solstice, the time when Jephthah offered his daughter as a sacrifice, and his knife began to bleed. On these four days of

[11] Another translation of *Tanhuma B* 5-7 is found in "Jephthah and His Daughter," in Hayim Nahman Bialik and Yehoshua Hana Ravnitzky, eds., *The Book of Legends: Sefer Ha-Aggadah* (New York: Schocken Books, 1992) 109.

[12] Louis Ginzberg, *The Legends of the Jews* (Philadelphia: Jewish Publication Society of America, 1913) 4:204.

the turn of the sun the maidens of Israel went to lament Jephthah's daughter. According to some authorities, however, the poisoned state of the water during the four turns of the sun is due to different causes.

### *Exodus Rabbah* 15:4 (twelfth century)[13]

"[L]eaping upon the mountains" for "mountains" refers to ancestors, as it says: Hear, O ye mountains, the LORD's controversy (Micah 6:2). R. Nehemiah gave another interpretation of "leaping upon the mountains": God said, "Israel have no good deeds to their credit to warrant redemption, only the merit of their elders," as it says: Go, and gather the elders of Israel together (Exod 3:16); and "mountains" refers to the elders, for so does the daughter of Jephthah say to her father: That I may go down upon the mountains (Judg 11:37). Did she then go upon the mountains? No, she went to the elders to prove to them that she was a pure virgin.

### *Numbers Rabbah* 19:15 (twelfth century)[14]

This fact teaches that the whole book breathes the Holy Spirit, for among all the judges there was none less esteemed than Jephthah.

### *Chronicles of Jerahmeel* [15]

She went off with her companions to "shed my tears and thus soften the grief of my youth." She was submissive about her father's vow, but felt she might not be worthy. God gave her assurance "her death shall be very precious in My sight." . . . Seila "fell upon her mother's bosom" and went to lament her faith.

---

[13] *Midrash Rabbah: Exodus,* ed. H. Freedman and Maurice Simon (London: Soncino, 1939) 163.

[14] *Midrash Rabbah: Numbers,* ed. H. Freedman and Maurice Simon (London: Soncino, 1939), 765.

[15] Date for *Chronicles of Jerahmeel* is unavailable. Quoted in Phyllis Silverman Kramer, "Jephthah's Daughter: A Thematic Approach to the Narrative as Seen in Selected Rabbinic Exegesis and in Artwork," in Athalya Brenner, ed., *A Feminist Companion to the Bible. Judges* (Sheffield: Sheffield Academic Press, 1999) 72. Note that unlike the text in Ps.-Philo 40:6-7, where Seila laments her fate, here she laments her faith.

## The Daughter of Jephtha the Gileadite.
## Peter Abelard (1079–1142)[16]

Come ye celibate virgins, as is wont,
To the solemn dances in a ring!
    As is wont let there be mournful songs
    And laments in the way of solemn hymns!
Let sad faces be unadorned,
    Like (the faces) of those that lament and weep!
    Let gold embroidered robes of state [ciclades] be absent,
    And rich ornaments be laid aside!
The maiden daughter of Jephtha, the Gileadite,
    Made the pitiful victim of her father,
    Demands the yearly elegies (sung by) virgins
    And the melodies of pious song,
    Due to the virtue of the maiden from year to year.
O maid, more to be admired than lamented!
O how seldom may a man be found like unto her!
    Let not a father's vow be ineffectual,
    And let not one defraud the LORD (of) a promise
    Who through him (the father) saved a people.
    She urges him (her father) against her own throat.
What more, what farther may we say?
Why tears, why utter lamentations?
    Yet to its end that which we have undertaken
    Lamenting and weeping we bring.
With her garments gathered about her,
    On the steps of the kindled altar,
    By her herself the sword is delivered (to her father).
    He saw her on her bended knees.
O frenzied mind of a judge
O mad zeal of a prince!
    O father, yet enemy of his kin,
    Which he destroyed by the slaughter of his only daughter!
Tell it aloud, ye virgin daughters of the Hebrews,
    Mindful of the exalted maid;
    Ye illustrious daughters of Israel,
    Rightly noble through this virgin!

---

[16] The story of Jephthah's daughter appears rarely in medieval Christian writings. Abelard's poem is critical of Jephthah's vow while praising the daughter's sacrifice. Her sacrifice exceeds that of many men. Reinforcing the horror of her death is the detail that she presents the implement of death, a sword, to her father. The women are told to pass on the story of the "noble" daughter. Peter Abelard, "The Daughter of Jephtha the Gileadite," in

## David Kimhi (1160–1235)[17]

It is quite clear that he did not kill her because the text (vs. 37) does not say, "I will mourn for my life," [but only "I will mourn for my virginity"]. This indicates that he did not kill her but rather that she did not know a man [remained a virgin], because the text says, "She did not know a man." Furthermore, the text (vs. 39) goes on to say "he fulfilled with her the vow which he made. It does not say that he offered her up as a burnt offering. He built her a house and placed her there. She became a recluse from mankind and from the ways of the world."

## *Rain Falls on the Mountaintop* (2001). Alicia Ostriker[18]

> She has no name, has neither face nor eyes
> they were drowned in blood
> they were burnt
> by fire
> She is a garden shut, a fountain sealed
> She sought her beloved and found him not
> no kisses of the mouth no child at breast
> no belly of heaped wheat
> she is the song of nothing
> and never
> She loved the man she called father
> a great a mighty warrior
> a rock an outstretched arm his enemies fled
> she ran after his love she praised she danced
> hallelujah father but he
> was angry
> He said she hurt him, she caused him grief
> he took her she consented he raised the knife
> she lay on stone and showed her throat she said
> blessed be he who protects and saves
> who comforts the captive and raises up
> the dead

---

Wilber Owen Sypherd, *Jephthah and His Daughter: A Study in Comparative Literature* (Newark: University of Delaware, 1948) 9–10.

[17] David Marcus, *Jephthah and His Vow* (Lubbock, TX: Texas Tech Press, 1986) 8. Marcus discusses other Christian references to Judges 11.

[18] Alicia Ostriker, "Jephthah's Daughter: A Lament," in Jane Schaberg, Alice Bach, and Esther Fuchs, eds., *On the Cutting Edge: The Study of Women in Biblical Worlds* (New York: Continuum, 2003) 240–41.

Her father will die at a good old age
but where was the angel to stop his hand
where was the sacred messenger
who is this God of stone and knife and fire
why does he hide, what can he see
when a woman prays
Will he ever hear
from the forest of our lives
into the clearing
rain falls on the mountaintop
soaking the wordless stone
year after year
like the truth of tears

# BIBLIOGRAPHY

Ackerman, Susan. *Warrior, Dancer, Seductress, Queen: Women in Judges and Biblical Israel.* New York: Doubleday, 1998.

Adler, Rachel. *Engendering Judaism: An Inclusive Theology and Ethics.* Boston: Beacon, 1998.

Amit, Yairah. *Reading Biblical Narratives: Literary Criticism and the Hebrew Bible.* Minneapolis: Fortress, 2001.

Aquino, María Pilar, ed. "Latina Feminist Theology: Central Features," in eadem, ed., *A Reader in Latina Feminist Theology: Religion and Justice.* Austin: University of Texas Press, 2002.

*Babylonian Talmud.* 18 vols. Translated into English with notes, glossary, and indices under the editorship of I[sidore] Epstein. London: Soncino, 1935–48.

Bal, Mieke. *Death & Dissymmetry: The Politics of Coherence in the Book of Judges.* Chicago: University of Chicago Press, 1988.

Barton, John. "Source Criticism," in David Noel Freedman, ed., *The Anchor Bible Dictionary (ABD).* New York: Doubleday, 1992. 6:162.

Bialik, Hayim Nahman and Yeshoshua Hana Ravnitzky, eds. *Book of Legends: Sefer Ha-Aggadah: Legends From the Talmud and Midrash.* New York: Schocken Books, 1992.

Bird, Phyllis. *Missing Persons and Mistaken Identities: Women and Gender in Ancient Israel.* Minneapolis: Fortress, 1997.

———. "Women (OT)" *ABD* 6:951–57.

Boling, Robert G. *Judges.* AB 6A. Garden City, NY: Doubleday, 1975.

Boyarin, Daniel. *Intertextuality and the Reading of Midrash.* Bloomington: Indiana University Press, 1994.

Bronner, Leila Leah. *From Eve to Esther: Rabbinic Reconstructions of Biblical Women.* Louisville: Westminster John Knox, 1994.

Brown, Cheryl Anne. *No Longer Be Silent: First Century Jewish Portraits of Biblical Women.* Louisville: Westminster John Knox, 1992.

Cross, Frank Moore. *Canaanite Myth and Hebrew Epic: Essays in the Religion of Israel.* Cambridge: Harvard University Press, 1973.

Daly, Mary. *Beyond God the Father: Toward a Philosophy of Women's Liberation.* Boston: Beacon, 1973.

Darr, Katheryn Pfisterer. "More than Historical Criticism: Critical, Rabbinical, and Feminist Perspectives on Biblical Interpretation," in eadem, *Far More Pre-*

*cious than Jewels: Perspectives on Biblical Women*. Louisville: Westminster John Knox, 1991.

Day, Peggy. "From the Child is Born the Woman: The Story of Jephthah's Daughter," in eadem, *Gender and Difference in Ancient Israel*. Minneapolis: Fortress, 1989, 58–74.

Exum, J. Cheryl. *Fragmented Women: Feminist (Sub)versions of Biblical Narratives*. Valley Forge, PA: Trinity Press International, 1993.

———. "On Judges 11," in Athalya Brenner, ed., *A Feminist Companion to Judges*. Sheffield: Sheffield Academic Press, 1993, 131–44.

———. *Tragedy and Biblical Narrative*. Cambridge: Cambridge University Press, 1992.

Friedman, Richard Elliot. *The Exile and Biblical Narrative: The Formation of the Deuteronomistic and Priestly Works*. Chico: Scholars, 1981.

Frymer-Kensky, Tikva. *Reading the Women of the Bible: A New Interpretation of Their Stories*. New York: Schocken Books, 2002.

Fuchs, Esther. *Sexual Politics of the Biblical Narrative: Reading the Hebrew Bible as a Woman*. Sheffield: Sheffield Academic Press, 2000.

———. "Marginalization, Ambiguity, Silencing: The Story of Jephthah's Daughter." *Journal of Feminist Studies in Religion* (Spring 1989) 35–45.

*Genesis Rabbah: The Judaic Commentary to the Book of Genesis*. Ed. Jacob Neusner. Atlanta: Scholars, 1985.

Gersh, Harry. *Talmud: Law and Commentary*. West Orange, NJ: Behrman House, 1986.

———. *Mishnah: The Oral Law*. West Orange, NJ: Behrman House, 1984.

Ginzberg, Louis. *The Legends of the Jews*. 7 vols. Philadelphia: Jewish Publication Society of America, 1913.

Goldenberg, Naomi. *Changing of the Gods*. Boston: Beacon, 1979.

Goldenberg, Robert. "Talmud," in Barry W. Holtz, ed., *Back to the Sources: Reading the Classical Jewish Texts*. New York: Summit Books, 1984.

Goldstein, Elyse. *ReVisions: Seeing Torah Through a Feminist Lens*. Woodstock, VT: Jewish Lights, 1998.

Hackett, Jo Ann. "In the Days of Jael: Reclaiming the History of Women in Ancient Israel," in Clarissa W. Atkinson, Constance H. Buchanan, and Margaret R. Miles, eds., *Immaculate and Powerful*. Boston: Beacon, 1985, 15–38.

Hallote, Rachel S. *Death, Burial, and Afterlife in the Biblical World*. Chicago: Ivan R. Dee, 2001.

Halpern-Amaru, Betsy. "Portraits of Women in Pseudo-Philo's Biblical Antiquities," in Amy-Jill Levine, ed., *"Women Like This": New Perspectives on Jewish Women in the Greco-Roman World*. Atlanta: Scholars, 1991, 83–106.

Hammer, Reuven. *The Classic Midrash*. New York: Paulist, 1995.

Herr, Larry G., and Douglas R. Clark. "Excavating the Tribe of Reuben." *Biblical Archaeological Review* (March/April 2001) 36–47.

Holladay, Carl H. "Biblical Criticism," *Harper's Bible Dictionary*. San Francisco: HarperSanFrancisco, 1985, 129–33.

Holladay, William L. *The Psalms Through Three Thousand Years*. Minneapolis: Fortress, 1993.

Holtz, Barry W. "Midrash," in idem, ed., *Back to the Sources: Reading the Classical Jewish Texts*. New York: Summit Books, 1984, 177–211.

Hyman, Naomi M. *Biblical Women in the Midrash: A Sourcebook*. Northvale, NJ: Jason Aronson, 1998.

Isasi-Díaz, Ada María. *Mujerista Theology*. Maryknoll, NY: Orbis, 1996.

Josephus, Flavius. *Antiquities of the Jews*. In *The Works of Josephus*. Trans. William Whiston. Peabody, MA: Hendrickson, 1987.

Kramer, Phyllis Silverman. "Jephthah's Daughter: A Thematic Approach to the Narrative as Seen in Selected Rabbinic Exegesis and in Artwork," in Athalya Brenner, ed., *A Feminist Companion to the Bible. Judges*. Sheffield: Sheffield Academic Press, 1999, 67–92.

Lerner, Gerda. *The Creation of Feminist Consciousness: From the Middle Ages to Eighteen-Seventy*. New York: Oxford University Press, 1993.

———. *The Creation of Patriarchy*. New York: Oxford University Press, 1993.

Levenson, Jon D. *The Death and Resurrection of the Beloved Son*. New Haven: Yale University Press, 1993.

McCarthy, David. "Reading the Bible Up Close and Personal." Unpublished manuscript.

Marcus, David. *Jephthah and His Vow*. Lubbock, TX: Texas Tech Press, 1986.

Meyers, Carol L. "Gender Roles and Genesis 3:16 Revisited," in Athalya Brenner and Carol Fontaine, eds., *A Feminist Companion to Genesis*. Sheffield: Sheffield Academic Press, 1997, 118–41.

———. *Rediscovering Eve: Ancient Israelite Women in Context*. New York: Oxford University Press, 1988.

*Midrash Rabbah*. 10 vols. Translated into English with notes, glossary and indices under the editorship of H[arry] Freedman and Maurice Simon, with a foreword by I[sidore] Epstein. London: Soncino, 1939; 1983.

*Midrash Tanhuma Yelammedenu*. Ed. Samuel A Berman. Hoboken, NJ: Ktav Publishing, 1996.

Miller, Barbara B. "Women, Death and Mourning in the Ancient Eastern Mediterranean World." Ph.D. diss., University of Michigan. Ann Arbor: University Microfilms International, 1994.

Milne, Pamela. "Toward Feminist Companionship: The Future of Feminist Biblical Studies and Feminism," in Athalya Brenner and Carole Fontaine, eds., *A Feminist Companion to Reading the Bible*. Sheffield: Sheffield Academic Press, 1997, 39–60.

*The Mishnah: A New Translation*. Trans. Jacob Neusner. New Haven: Yale University Press, 1988.

Neusner, Jacob. *Introduction to Rabbinic Literature*. New York: Doubleday, 1994.

———. *Judaism and Scripture: The Evidence of Leviticus Rabbah*. Chicago: University of Chicago Press, 1986.

Ochshorn, Judith. *The Female Experience and the Nature of the Divine*. Bloomington: Indiana University Press, 1981.

Ostriker, Alicia. "Jephthah's Daughter: A Lament," in Jane Schaberg, Alice Bach, and Esther Fuchs, eds., *On the Cutting Edge: The Study of Women in Biblical Worlds*. New York: Continuum, 2003, 230–49.

Patai, Raphael. *Gates to the Old City: A Book of Jewish Legends*. Northvale, NJ: Jason Aronson, 1980.

Patterson, Stephen J. *The God of Jesus: The Historical Jesus & the Search for Meaning*. Harrisburg: Trinity Press International, 1998.

Plaskow, Judith. "Dealing with Difference Without and Within," *Journal of Feminist Studies in Religion* (Spring 2003) 91–95, Vol. 19.

———. "The Coming of Lilith: Toward a Feminist Theology," in Carol P. Christ and Judith Plaskow, eds., *Womenspirit Rising: A Feminist Reader in Religion*. San Francisco: Harper & Row, 1979, 198–209.

Plaut, W. Gunther. *The Torah: A Modern Commentary*. New York: Union of American Hebrew Congregations, 1981.

Pseudo-Philo. In James H. Charlesworth, ed., *The Old Testament Pseudepigrapha*. Garden City, NY: Doubleday, 1985, 2:297–377.

Rabinowitz, Louis Isaac. "Vows and Vowing," *Encyclopaedia Judaica*. Jerusalem: Kater Publishing, 1972, Vol. 16, 227.

Rattray, Susan. "Worship," *Harper's Bible Dictionary*. San Francisco: HarperSanFrancisco, 1985, 1143–47.

Reinhartz, Adele. *"Why Ask My Name?" Anonymity and Identity in Biblical Narrative*. New York: Oxford University Press, 1998.

Römer, Thomas C. "Why Would the Deuteronomists Tell About the Sacrifice of Jephthah's Daughter?" *JSOT* 77 (1998) 27–38.

Rosenberg, A. J. *Judges: A New Translation*. New York: Judaica Press, 1987.

Rosenberg. Joel. "Bible: Biblical Narrative," in Barry W. Holtz, ed., *Back to the Sources: Reading the Classic Jewish Texts*. New York: Summit Books, 1984, 31–81.

Ruether, Rosemary Radford. *Womanguides: Readings Toward a Feminist Theology*. Boston: Beacon, 1985.

Schneider, Tammi J. *Judges*. Berit Olam: Studies in Hebrew Narrative and Poetry. Collegeville: Liturgical Press, 2000.

Schüssler Fiorenza, Elisabeth. *Wisdom Ways: Introducing Feminist Biblical Interpretation*. Maryknoll, NY: Orbis, 2001.

Schwartz, Howard. *Reimagining the Bible: The Storytelling of the Rabbis*. New York: Oxford University Press, 1998.

Shapiro, Rona. "Woman's Life, Woman's Truth," in Elyse Goldstein, ed., *The Woman's Torah Commentary*. Woodstock, VT: Jewish Lights, 2000, 70–78.

Sölle, Dorothee, Joe H. Kirchberger, and Herbert Haag. *Great Women of the Bible in Art and Literature*. Grand Rapids: Eerdmans, 1994.

Stanton, Elizabeth Cady. *The Woman's Bible*. Boston: Northeastern University Press, 1993.

Steinberg, Naomi. "Social Scientific Criticism: Judges 9 and Issues of Kinship," in Gale R. Yee, ed., *Judges and Method: New Approaches in Biblical Studies*. Minneapolis: Fortress, 1995, 45–64.

Sypherd, Wilber Owen. *Jephthah and His Daughter: A Study in Comparative Literature.* Newark: University of Delaware Press, 1948.

*Targum Jonathan of the Former Prophets.* Trans. Daniel J. Harrington and Anthony J. Saldarini. Wilmington: Michael Glazier, 1987.

Telushkin, Joseph. *The Book of Jewish Values.* New York: Bell Tower, 2000.

Trible, Phyllis. *Texts of Terror.* Philadelphia: Fortress, 1984.

———. "A Love Story Gone Awry," in eadem, *God and the Rhetoric of Sexuality.* Philadelphia: Fortress, 1978, 72–143.

Valler, Shulamit. "The Story of Jephthah's Daughter in the Midrash," in Athalya Brenner, ed., *A Feminist Companion to Judges.* Sheffield: Sheffield Academic Press, 1999, 48–66.

Van Gennep, Arnold. *The Rites of Passage.* Chicago: University of Chicago Press, 1960.

van Wolde, Ellen. "Intertextuality: Ruth in Dialogue with Tamar," in Athalya Brenner and Carole Fontaine, eds., *A Feminist Companion to Reading the Bible.* Sheffield: Sheffield Academic Press, 1997, 426–51.

Walker, Alice. *In Search of Our Mothers' Gardens.* New York: Harcourt, Brace, Jovanovich, 1983.

Walsh, Jerome T. *Style and Structure in Biblical Hebrew Narrative.* Collegeville: Liturgical Press, 2001.

Weems, Renita J. *Battered Love: Marriage, Sex, and Violence in the Hebrew Prophets.* Minneapolis: Fortress, 1995.

———. *Just a Sister Away: A Womanist Vision of Women's Relationhips in the Bible.* San Diego: LuraMedia, 1988.

Williams, Delores S. *Sisters in the Wilderness: The Challenge of Womanist God-Talk.* Maryknoll, NY: Orbis, 1993.

Yee, Gale R., ed. *Judges and Method: New Approaches in Biblical Studies.* Minneapolis: Fortress, 1995.

# INDEX OF SUBJECTS

# INDEX OF SCRIPTURE

## New Testament